# LIBERATOR ALBUM

B-24 Liberators
of the 2nd Air Division
USAAF

This book is dedicated to the memory
of my good friend William ('Bill') Robertie,
who worked so very hard on behalf of the
2nd Air Division Association.

**Liberator Album**
Mike Bailey with Tony North. 

ISBN 1 85780 060 5

First published in 1998 by
Midland Publishing Limited
24 The Hollow, Earl Shilton,
Leicester, LE9 7NA, England
Tel: 01455 847 256 Fax: 01455 841 805
E-mail: midlandbooks@compuserve.com

*Worldwide distribution (except North America):*
Midland Counties Publications (Aerophile) Limited
Unit 3, Maizefield, Hinckley Fields
Hinckley, Leics., LE10 1YF, England
Telephone: 01455 233 747 Fax: 01455 233 737
E-mail: midlandbooks@compuserve.com

*North American trade distribution:*
Specialty Press Publishers & Wholesalers Inc
11481 Kost Dam Road, North Branch, MN 55056, USA
Tel: 612 583 3239 Fax: 612 583 2023
Toll free telephone: 800 895 4585

Design concept and editorial layout
© Midland Publishing Limited
and Stephen Thompson Associates

Edited by Ken Ellis

Printed and bound in Italy by
LEGO SpA.
Jacket printed in England



*Half-title page:*
**B-24H-1-CF 41-29126 *Conquest Cavalier* of the 701st Bomb Squadron, cruises over scattered cloud in the spring of 1944. This was one of the 96th Combat Bomb Wing, 445th Bombardment Group's original aircraft.**
(See Chapter Two)

*Title page:*
**Amid the mud of the newly-completed Shipdham airfield, the 14th Combat Bomb Wing's 44th Bombardment Group – *The Flying Eightballs* – taxi out for a training mission. The aircraft in the foreground proudly carries the Group's insignia on the port side of the nose.**

# LIBERATOR ALBUM

## B-24 Liberators of the 2nd Air Division USAAF

Mike Bailey with Tony North

Midland Publishing Limited

# Preface

My love affair with the Consolidated B-24 Liberator developed back in 1944 when I and a school chum, both impressionable, aeroplane-mad ten year olds, living in Norwich – the very heart of Liberator country – spent numerous Saturdays trespassing on our nearest airfield, Horsham St Faith.

After stealthily negotiating a hedge and traversing a couple of fields we would find ourselves on the dispersal area of the 458th Bomb Group's 754th Squadron and, thanks to the good natured tolerance of the air and ground crews we came in contact with, we spent may happy hours clambering through the various B-24s parked there, while witnessing at close quarters all the activities of an air base at war.

Even at that tender age, the outward differences in the various Liberator models were not lost on us and many years later when my interest in aviation blossomed again, it was those memories, now deeply etched into my mind, which prompted me to delve into the B-24's history. Sometime in the 1960s I started to compile a collection of photographs of 2nd Air Division Liberators acquired both from official sources and private individuals.

As is often the case, what started out as an interesting hobby soon grew into an obsession and in the early 1970s I happened to meet, by chance, Tony North at Seething. During our conversation he expressed a keen interest in the very subject which had obsessed me over the years – the B-24 Liberator. Very soon we found ourselves pooling resources, photograph collections and information on the Bomb Groups of the 2nd Air Division.

Back in 1974, I met up with (the now late) 'Bill' Robertie, a former President of the 2nd Air Division Association, who made me an Honorary member of the Association, which, in turn brought me into contact with many veteran Liberator crewmen, lots of whom made their photographs available to Tony and myself.

Sometime later Tony and I discussed the feasibility of compiling a series of softback books containing some of our photographs, covering the bomb groups that comprised the 2nd Air Division. We decided to go ahead with the first volume, with Tony doing the photograph layout and captions and myself executing the front cover painting and the colour 'Lib' profiles in the centre spread.

Volume One (published privately in 1979) dealt with the 20th Combat Bomb Wing (CBW) and was received with considerable enthusiasm by the aviation aficionados, and the encouraging reviews we received prompted us to go ahead with two more volumes – the next, published in 1981, we devoted to the 14th CBW, and the third, featuring the 96th CBW, appeared in 1984.

Some years had passed since the publication of the third volume and we were getting quite a bit of urging from enthusiasts to prepare Volume Four, which was to cover the 2nd CBW. By this time, the first three volumes had become collectors' items.

Unfortunately Tony developed a severe medical condition affecting his eyes during this period which made any contribution towards captioning and photograph layout just about impossible for him.

As the demand for a fourth volume continued to grow, I decided to compile this on my own and so went ahead with the task of photograph selection, captioning, preparing the colour sideviews and cover painting.

It was nearly complete when Chris Salter of Midland Publishing contacted me and suggested they produce a new hardback book in their classic format, featuring the best of the three earlier volumes (including additional photographs received since their publication) – plus the newly prepared material for the 'missing' fourth volume.

The result of all this you have in your hands and I sincerely hope it brings you pleasure.

I apologise in advance for any inaccuracies incurred in its compilation and I thank all the many friends both in this country and in the USA who have supplied material and encouragement throughout the history of the project.

# Acknowledgements

Over the years many individuals and organisations, in England and in the United States have contributed towards the creation of this book by making available photographs, information and much encouragement. To all go my heartfelt thanks.

To the following individuals: Steve Adams, George Alexander, Tom Allan, John Archer, Christine Armes, W D Beauregard, Allen G Blue, Phyliss du Bois, Martin Bowman, Chaz Bowyer, Fred R Breuninger, Tom Brittain, Bill Cameron, Bob Coleman, Gerry Collins, Phil Day, Pat Everson, Roger Freeman, Peter Frost, Charles Freudenthal, Chriss Gotts, Steve Gotts, William Green, Carl Gjelhaug, Ursel P Harvell, David Hastings, Ian Hawkins, Herman Hetzel, George Higgins, Harry Holmes, Calvin Horn, James Hoseason, Everett R Jones, Myron Keilman, Tony Kerrison, Jim Kiernan and his wife Sharon D Vance Kiernan (the original *Sharon D*), Tom Kinnally, David Klaus, Ron Kramer, Larry van Kuran, Sean Leahy, Will Lundy, Ian McLachlan, William T Larkins, John McNany, David Mayor, Danny Moore, Allison D Myfield, Wiley Noble, Tony North, Ted Parker, Pat Ramm, 'Bill' Robertie, Rick Rokicki, George Reynolds, Charles C Russell, Ed Scharm, Jonathan Smith, Erdie B Stevens, Bob Vickers.

Thanks are also due to the 2nd Air Division Association, the International Liberator Club, the Swedish government, the Swiss Air Force and to the US Army and US Air Force. Also to Ken Ellis for his sound advice.

And of course special thanks are due to my long-suffering wife, Maureen, for her resigned patience in tolerating my mad obsession and for providing refreshment for the countless 8th Air Force 'vets' and local enthusiasts visiting our humble abode through the years.

Mike Bailey
Norwich, Norfolk December 1997

# Contents



---

*Jacket illustration:*
A 2nd Air Division formation scene
from a painting by Mike Bailey.

JU
JU
L
H

294932
+C

Chapter One

# 2nd Air Division Liberators

The technical development and production of the Consolidated B-24 Liberator is a very complex and detailed story which has been well covered in previous books. Allen G Blue, Martin Bowman and Roger Freeman have all produced excellent accounts of the technical and operational prowess of the bomber and their books are highly recommended for those wishing to delve more deeply into the subject (see the Bibliography).

This volume is intended as a visual feast for the aviation enthusiast, historian, Liberator veteran or model maker and the myriad complexities of the aircraft's evolution and development have no place here. However, a brief resumé of the Liberators flown within the 2nd Air Division (AD) will help clarify certain points not immediately apparent to the uninitiated.

Informative captions have been attached to each photograph, giving where possible the aircraft's serial number and production block number. For the period of B-24 production, United States Army Air Force (USAAF) serial numbers constituted a two-digit prefix followed by a sequential number of between two and six digits. The two-digit prefix represented the fiscal year in which the aircraft was ordered (although it was not necessarily built in that year) and the other figures are in effect the individual aircraft's serial number. For example, the B-24H 42-94932 of the 489th Bombardment Group's (BG) 846th Bomb Squadron (as illustrated on the opposite page) lay within a batch of 228 B-24Hs ordered in fiscal year 1942 from Ford. On the aircraft, the fiscal year was abbreviated to the last digit (in this case '2') and appended to the aircraft's serial number without the hyphen – hence on *Paper Doll* it appeared as 294932.

By the time the 8th Air Force were operating the Liberator no less than five production plants in the USA were turning out the bomber. Within the designation of the aircraft, each manufacturing plant was given a two-letter suffix code as follows:

| | | |
|---|---|---|
| -CF | Consolidated | Fort Worth, Texas |
| -CO | Consolidated | San Diego, California |
| -DT | Douglas | Tulsa, Oklahoma |
| -FO | Ford | Willow Run, Michigan |
| -NT | N'th American | Dallas, Texas |

To continue using *Paper Doll* 42-94932 as the example, its full designation is as follows: B-24H-20-FO. The 'B' puts it in the bomber category which was initiated in 1924 and still in use, the latest recipient of the prefix is the Northrop Grumman B-2A Spirit 'stealth' bomber. Each type ordered was given a sequential number, the B-24 Liberator being the 24th type of bomber to be adopted. (Before the B-24 came the Douglas B-23 Dragon, after came the famous North American B-25 Mitchell.)

The 'H' suffix relates to the specific model number, an evolving system of variants, of which more later. The '-20' is the aircraft's block number, a system introduced in 1941 to denote equipment changes between production blocks, ie the place on the production track where a new equipment fit was initiated. There are variations within the system, but for B-24s, these ran -1, -5, 10 and then in fives upwards. The largest block numbers could be found within the B-24J series, with Consolidated machines going as far as -210s although the small batch of -401s appear to defy an otherwise logical system. Thus *Paper Doll* is within the fifth production block change for the B-24H undertaken at Willow Run, the latter revealed from the already noted -FO suffix.

The first three Bomb Groups assigned to the 2nd Air Division – the 44th, 93rd and 389th were all initially equipped with the B-24D version of the Liberator. The 'D was the first really effective high altitude bomber version of the 'Lib' with its Pratt & Whitney R-1830 engines each giving 1,200hp (895kW) and fitted with turbo-superchargers to aid high altitude performance. The earlier production 'Ds serving with the 44th and 93rd Groups carried a defensive armament of ten heavy calibre 0.50 machine guns with two in the Martin top turret, two in the Consolidated tail turret, three flexible hand-held weapons in the nose, one at each waist window and one in the rear under belly hatch.

Once these groups started flying missions it was realised that the 'Libs' were rather vulnerable to head-on attacks and steps were taken to improve defensive armament in the nose section with the central nose gun often repositioned slightly higher and in many cases doubled up with an extra gun. This improved things a bit but made for a very cluttered nose section with extra guns and ammunition belts impeding the bombardier at his work. Many of the later B-24Ds arriving at Hethel with the 389th Bomb Group in the summer of 1943 carried a Briggs/Sperry ventral ball turret with twin guns thus eliminating the hand-held rear belly gun.

In mid-1943, while the three B-24D-equipped groups were on detachment in North Africa, a new group, the 392nd arrived at Wendling bringing over new models of the B-24 equipped with power turrets in the nose. The vast majority of these new aircraft were Ford-built B-24Hs with a few Consolidated-built 'J versions thrown in. The nose turrets certainly were more efficient in protecting the bombers from the head-on attacks but their added weight, the reduced streamlining and the shift in the centre of gravity made these new aircraft a little slower and also that bit more difficult to hold in a tight formation at altitude.

The turrets also drastically reduced the forward view for the bombardier and navigator. The pilot and co-pilot also suffered as their view forward over the nose – not good even in the 'D model – was reduced even further by the bulky turret standing up above the natural nose contour, not to mention the astrodome and pitot head masts which also obscured forward visibility.

These new 'H and 'J models were all equipped with the ball turret which could be retracted into the belly when not in use. The 'H and 'J models varied from each other quite considerably in a number of

*Opposite page:*

*Top:* **Pathfinder aircraft of the 446th Bomb Group carried a circle marking on the tail denoting their role. B-24L-5-FO 44-49355 'JU-L' of the 446th Bombardment Group's 707th Bomb Squadron drops bombs and smoke-markers over Landsberg on 9th April 1945. Note the hand-held tail gun mounting fitted to some B-24Ls and B-24H-30-FO 42-95289 *Little Rollo* in the background.**

*Bottom:* **At rest in the Suffolk sun at Halesworth is B-24H-20-FO (42-94932) *Paper Doll* of the 846th BS, 489th BG, along with *Stubby Gal* B-24H-20-FO (42-94836) in the background. *Paper Doll* crashed after colliding with 42-94888 on return from Kassel on 27th September 1944.**

ways including different bomb sights and autopilots with the 'H models carrying the Sperry S-1 bomb sight with the A-5 autopilot and the 'Js were equipped with the Norden M-9 bomb sight and the C-1 autopilot.

The obvious outward sign of difference between the early 'Hs and 'Js was in the nose turret, the 'Js carrying the Consolidated and later the Motor Products nose turrets which were angled at the front and heavily metalled at the sides, whilst the 'Hs were equipped with the roomier and more efficient Emerson turret which had smoother contours and used much more Plexiglas in its construction.

The bombardier's transparency also differed, with that in the 'H angled back beneath the nose section more than that of the 'J. Most of the production plants standardised on this type of nose section later in the war. In an effort to improve visibility for the navigator and bombardier new types of blister windows were devised and field fitted into the sides of Liberator noses, with these innovations later incorporated on the production lines. Very few North American-built 'Js saw service in the 8th, and it was a very rare 'bird' indeed in England.

Another problem was caused by the sub-zero slipstream rushing into the rear fuselage through the open waist gun windows, causing the gunners extreme discomfort and in many cases frostbite. Ford tackled this problem and in May of 1944 new 'Hs arriving in the UK had flush Plexiglass waist windows replacing the hinged hatches. The gun was now placed in a swivel mount below the window. These windows were deepened in later production batches with the gun-mount incorporated into the window itself. Later on, field kits were supplied to the bases in the form of a framed bay window with a central gun-mount to be field-fitted to the older 'Libs' with the open windows. This was attached over the existing open hatch.

By the summer of 1944 it was felt that sufficient escort fighter groups were now available to give added protection to the bombers all the way to their targets, and it was decided by the high command that the weighty, drag-inducing ball turrets should be removed from the 'Libs'. This order was delivered to the groups in July of 1944 but was not always carried out, as the hard-pressed ground crews had more urgent tasks in hand and it was often several months before these turrets were removed. Several Liberators still carried ball turrets at the end of the war, as some group commanders found it prudent to have ball-turreted B-24s strategically placed throughout the formation at vulnerable positions.

As the war progressed it was decided to remove bomb sights from most B-24s with the sights being retained only by special lead and deputy lead ships who would release their bombs accompanied by a smoke marker which would leave a trail of white smoke in the sky. The rest of the formation would release their bombs on this signal. Group and squadron lead ships were now seen with H2X radomes in the ball turret well. Another innovation was the addition to many aircraft of Plexiglas blisters beneath the nose containing the 'Fishhook' aerials for the 'Carpet Blinker' radio countermeasure sets.

By the summer of 1944 most of the production centres had standardised on the Emerson nose turret but Consolidated at San Diego continued to use the Motor Products turret whilst many of their 'Js incorporated a new thermal de-icing system, dispensing with the black rubber de-icer boots on the leading edges of wings and tail surfaces.

The winter of 1944 saw a new model arriving from the USA this was the Ford-built 'L which featured a new lightweight power-operated tail gun cupola instead of the weighty turret. The twin guns were hand-held in this model and the gunner sat within the fuselage and this innovation saved several hundred pounds in weight. It was decided to use most of these 'L models as H2X 'Micky Ships'. The final version of the Liberator to reach the 8th Air Force was the B-24M, also produced by Fords, and very similar to the 'L but reverting to the normal tail turret.

In the final versions of the Ford-built 'L and in all the 'Ms, much larger, bulged, windows for the navigator were incorporated, also new bulged side-cockpit windows. Later versions of the 'M, a few of which reached the 8th Air Force just prior to the war's end had an entirely reworked cockpit transparency reducing the framing and incorporating a V-shaped windscreen making for improved visibility and an easier escape in an emergency.

Until April/May 1944, all the Liberators arriving in the UK for operations with the 8th Air Force were painted in dark olive drab on the upper surfaces and sides with neutral grey undersides but the style of finish was far from identical – each plant using a slightly differing style.

The demarcation line between the olive drab and the grey on B-24s produced by Consolidated at San Diego, Consolidated at Fort Worth and North American at Dallas was in a fairly regular curve along the length of the lower fuselage whilst those manufactured by Douglas at Tulsa had a slightly wavy division. This was taken a step further on the Ford production line with a much more exaggerated wave between the olive drab and the grey – this is a quick and easy means of identifying a Ford-built aircraft.

National insignia in the form of the dark blue disc with a white star was painted on the top surface of the port (left) wing and lower surface of the starboard (right) wing and on each side of the fuselage just forward, and on some models, slightly overlapping, the waist gun hatch. This fuselage insignia varied in both size and position with the various production batches of early 'Ds and 'H models carrying large insignia but reducing the size during the production run.

The Consolidated-built 'Js had smaller insignia from the start of their production – B-24Ds from the 93rd and 44th Bomb Groups were seen in the early days with a yellow border around the national insignia but this practise was soon discontinued and the yellow was painted out with dark olive drab or dark blue. About this time it was also deemed desirable to tone down the white stars and the national insignia was over sprayed in grey on most aircraft.

All Liberators had their serial numbers painted across their vertical stabilisers in deep yellow digits from 8-10in (20-25cm) high and beneath these, also in deep yellow, were added the aircraft radio call-letter. When B-24Ds of the 44th, 93rd and 389th BGs went on various detachments to North Africa they conformed to theatre requirements in having an RAF-style fin flash of red, white and blue added to their vertical stabilisers and these remained on the bombers after they returned to England.

A new style of national insignia was introduced in June of 1943 with a white bar added to each side of the blue disc with the whole emblem surrounded with a red border. In September of the same year a new order was received to overpaint the red with dark blue and this style was used from then on. It should be noted that in most cases these orders could not be acted on immediately as the ground crews usually had more pressing tasks to perform and it was often several weeks before all these paint jobs were carried out.

*Opposite page:*

*Top:* **The unmistakable planform of a B-24 Liberator. This olive drab example from the 445th Bombardment Group illustrates the wear and tear on the paint work, particularly on the leading edges and on the walkways for ground crew between the engines and over the fuselage. Note also the baffles on the waist gun positions; these helped to stem the effects of the freezing cold slipstream, but frostbite was still a frequent occurrence.**

*Bottom:* **With her wings flexing under a heavy load, *Skipper's Clipper* heads for the target. B-24H-20-FO 42-95000 served with the 701st Squadron of the 445th Bombardment Group. Note the wavy demarcation line between the olive drab and the grey – a hallmark of Ford-built B-24s.**

In June of 1943 new group markings were introduced to the 8th Air Force and those adopted by the 2nd AD Liberators comprised a white disc on the upper portion of the vertical tail surface and on the upper starboard wing of about 72in (1.8m) diameter. Superimposed on this disc would be the group's identification letter in insignia blue. The first group to sport this new insignia was the new 392nd Bomb Group at Wendling in August 1943. The other 2nd AD groups were in North Africa at this time and their new markings were applied when they arrived back in the UK shortly afterwards. When the white discs were applied to the tails the yellow serial numbers were repainted just below this disc with the call-letter on the lower portion of the fin.

In March of 1944 the Liberator groups applied two-character codes to the B-24 fuselages between the waist windows and the tail, a practise long in use with the RAF and the USAAF B-17 and fighter groups. These letters and numbers were originally intended to be 48in (1.2m) high but this ruling was never strictly adhered to and various sizes were used throughout the 2nd AD.

As the strength of the Division increased with additional groups arriving in the UK and larger formations setting out daily to do battle with the enemy, some problems with the group, wing and division assembly constantly plagued the missions. With bombers taking off from their bases at 30-second intervals and climbing through heavy cloud conditions to form their combat formations, usually in the murky light or an English dawn, difficulties were encountered in identifying their own combat wings and bomb groups.

To help ratify this situation an order was drafted in late April 1944 that all tailplanes be painted in a distinctive colour which would be easily identified in poor weather conditions and at a great distance, and by the end of May, the vast formations were enlivened by the vivid new plumage of their tail feathers. A further splash of colour,

added to the B-24s before the adoption of the new tail markings, was the vivid yellow bands painted along the lower portions of the bomb-bay doors to enable crews in combat to see if a companion's bomb-bay was in the open or closed position.

April and May 1944 saw new Liberators arriving in the UK completely devoid of camouflage paint apart from the olive drab anti-dazzle panels on the top surface of the nose section. This made the B-24 much lighter and saved quite a few man hours in the factories.

At first these shining examples stood out in stark contrast to their olive drab companions but gradually the situation changed as more and more of these silver birds replaced their older camouflaged sisters. On the natural metal aircraft it was decided, after a bit of experimenting with the white upper wing disc, to go over to a black disc with a white group letter and this was continued throughout the war.

Another measure adopted to help with group and wing assembly was the use of group assembly ships or 'Judas Goats' as they were called. These were usually old 'war weary' 'Libs' – often 'D models – which were painted in the most garish manner, easily identifiable by their parent bomb group. They would take-off from their field ahead of the rest of the group and circle in the group's assembly area flashing the recognition signal and firing flares until the complete bomb group was formed up behind. They would then usually return to their home base after the mission got on its way, although it has been known for various assembly ships to accompany their parent group to the target.

As the European war drew to a close the majority of B-24s throughout the division were the silvery natural metal models but quite a few of the battered old olive drab ships were still in evidence, patched and oil stained, but displaying their battle scars with pride.

*Top:* **A good view of the 453rd Bombardment Group tail markings prior to late May 1944 on B-24H-1-DT 41-28629. Noteworthy features of early 'H models are large national insignia, short rudder trim tabs and Consolidated rear turret with staggered guns.**

*Left:* **Just prior to the adoption of the coloured tailplanes some natural silver ships had black discs painted on their tails as a better means of identification than the white. B-24H-25-FO 42-95063 from the 389th Bombardment Group's 566th Bomb Squadron survived the hostilities.**

Chapter Two

# 2nd Combat Bomb Wing

*Above:* **The 389th BG's original aircraft were B-24Ds. B-24D-165-CO 42-72866, with ventral ball-turret retracted into the fuselage but with its twin guns pointing down and visible below the 'star-n-bar', is seen early in its combat career. 42-72866 was not at Hethel long before it acquired the name *Jackass Male* with a bomb totin' cartoon cowboy riding a jackass.**

## 389th BOMBARDMENT GROUP (H)
***The Sky Scorpions***

The 389th BG arrived at their base at Hethel in June and July 1943. Soon after this, the air echelon was sent on to North Africa to train for the low level mission against the Ploesti oil complex. After completing several combat missions from its Benghazi, Libya, base the 389th returned to the UK to fly its first mission from Hethel on 7th September 1943. The 389th was sent again on detachment to North Africa on 19th September and moved into the base at Massicault, Tunisia, for a couple of weeks, before returning again to the UK by 3rd October.

*The Sky Scorpions* dropped 17,548 tons of bombs on the enemy, lost 153 B-24s and claimed 209 enemy aircraft destroyed, 31 probables and 45 damaged. The group was awarded a Distinguished Unit Citation for the Ploesti mission and one of its pilots, 2nd/Lt Lloyd H Hughes, was posthumously awarded the Congressional Medal of Honor for his courage on that day.

**Group Markings**
The Group carried no group markings until the return to England after its first African adventure.

Then the 389th adopted a disc containing a capital 'C' on upper starboard wing (white on olive drab aircraft, black on the silver machines). The disc was repeated on outer vertical tail surfaces until May 1944 when tails were painted black with a white vertical stripe.

Squadron code letters were painted grey on olive drab, black on silver, as follows:

| | |
|---|---|
| 564th Squadron | 'YO -' |
| 565th Squadron | 'EE -' |
| 566th Squadron | 'RR -' |
| 567th Squadron | 'HP -' |

Many aircraft within the 389th also carried their individual call-letter (or call-sign) in yellow on the fuselage aft of the squadron codes.

From the autumn of 1943, 'bars' (minus signs) and 'plus' signs (+) were applied to the aircraft's individual call-letter on the fin/rudder. These squadron indicator markings were as follows:

| | |
|---|---|
| 564th Squadron | no sign |
| 565th Squadron | 'bar' before |
| 566th Squadron | '+' after |
| 567th Squadron | 'bar' after |

With the introduction of the all-black with white stripe tail, this changed to:

| | |
|---|---|
| 564th Squadron | no sign |
| 565th Squadron | 'bar' above |
| 566th Squadron | '+' below |
| 567th Squadron | 'bar' below |

*Above:* **High over a white-capped North Sea, 389th BG B-24D-15-CF 42-63960 climbs for altitude. Like many of the 2nd AD's B-24Ds, this machine had its frontal defence beefed-up with twin, hand-held guns in the bombardier's position. It also acquired 'boiler-plate' panels each side of the cockpit as protection for pilot and co-pilot. This Liberator force-landed at Ash, near Gravesend, Kent on return from a mission to Cognac-Chateaubernard on 31st December 1943 but was repaired and flown out from a temporary runway.**

*Left:* **Six thousand pounds of ordnance cascade from the bomb bays of B-24D-95-CO 42-40776 *Old Blister Butt* from the 389th's 564th BS. The RAF-style fin flashes on the inside vertical stabilisers were a legacy of its former service in North Africa where the US Liberator Groups were under RAF command. *Old Blister Butt* was later assigned to the 801st BG (P).**

*Above:* **B-24D-20-CF 42-63980 *Missouri Mauler* of the 567th BS, climbs to join up with the 389th BG's formation. This aircraft is one of the earlier B-24Ds which carried no ball-turret but had a single hand-held gun mounted in a port on the underside of the rear fuselage, just visible below the port vertical tail. *Missouri Mauler* was later assigned to the 801st BG (P).**

*Right:* **Target bound over 10/10ths undercast, 389th BG 566th BS B-24D-80-CO 42-40619 drones relentlessly onwards to its objective. The light coloured surround to the national insignia was red, photographic film of the time playing tricks. She belongs to the 566th BS. This 'Lib' was lost on the 24th February 1944 mission to Gotha.**

*Left:* **The 389th at bomb release, the nearest is B-24J-80-CO 42-100190 'J+' of the 566th BS. She was later named *Princess Konocti* and sported novel artwork of an Indian maiden each side of its nose section. The *Princess'* combat career came to an end when she had to force-land in Sweden at Halmstad on 20th June 1944 after the mission to Pölitz.**

*Below:* **With unlimited visibility over the continent of Europe, B24J-75-CO 42-100146 of the 389th's 564th BS, thunders its way to the target area. Typical of very early 'J models, it carried the Consolidated nose turret which featured staggered gun mountings, causing one gun barrel to protrude slightly further than the other. These early turrets soon gave way to the improved Motor Products turret on the Convair production line. Early 'Js also featured braced, horn-type pitot-tubes on the upper nose, soon to be replaced by lower mounted flush pitots. This aircraft was later transferred to the 567th BS and adopted the call-letter 'U+' and the name *Mistah Chick*.**

*Right:* **Close-up of nose of B-24D-120-CO 42-40997 *Screamin' Mimi*. The single hand-held nose gun was later replaced by twin guns in a slightly higher position in the bombardier's transparency (see the colour section). *Screamin' Mimi* later served with the 801st BG (P).**

*Below:* **Undergoing engine maintenance on its hardstand at Hethel, veteran B-24D-95-CO 42-40743 of the 389th's 567th BS displays 51 mission symbols on the 'boiler-plate' beneath the pilot's side window; the seventh symbol, painted horizontally, represents the low-level mission to Ploesti. By this time the red surround to the national insignia had been replaced by blue and the squadron code letters, 'HP' had been applied to the rear fuselage. Also of note is the yellow band along the lower section of the bomb doors – a visual aid to show others if the doors were open or closed. Eventually this aircraft was transferred out of the 389th BG and became the formation assembly ship for the 492nd BG, resplendent in white stripes.**

*Top: **Galloping Katie***, **B-24J-90-CO 42-100332 of the 566th BS was lost to the 389th BG on 16th March 1944 when she limped, in a damaged condition – note the No.4 propeller is feathered – into Dübendorf, Switzerland after the mission to Friedrichshafen.**

*Above: **My Tuffy*** **discards her ordnance over the target during the winter of 1943. B-24J-75-CO 42-100167 from the 566th BS was written off due to severe battle damage on 9th March 1944.**

*Top:* **Two of Hethel's early 'J models on their way to face the enemy. Nearest is B-24J-55-CO 42-99982 of the 566th, she crashed and burned after colliding with 392nd BG's 41-29485 over Foulsham on 9th April 1944.**

*Above:* **B-24J-130-CO 42-110084 *Don't Cry Baby* from the 389th's 565th BS was salvaged after crash-landing at Challock, Kent, on 17th July 1944.**

*Above:* **The months of April and May 1944 saw the arrival in the UK of the first unpainted, natural metal replacement Liberators. One of the very first of these, Convair-built B-24J-145-CO 44-40052, was assigned to the 389th BG and is illustrated in flight soon after its debut with the 565th Squadron. At first it was undecided how the tail markings should be displayed on the 'silver ships' and, as in this case, the outer tail surfaces were painted in standard olive drab with the white disc superimposed, as normal. This practice soon gave way to a solid black disc on the silver tail before the new black and white tail markings were adopted in late May 1944. 44-40052 soldiered on until it went missing on operations on 12th May 1945.**

*Below:* **Brand new B-24H-25-FO 42-95184 of the 389th's 567th BS demonstrating one of the Liberators most common ailments – nose wheel failure. This accident occurred during landing on 20th June 1944. Usually only minor damage occurred during these mishaps and '184 was repaired and went on to fly operations until she was lost on the Brunswick mission on 5th August 1944.**

*Left:* **Many of the 2nd Air Division Bomb Groups employed a Republic P-47 Thunderbolt as a formation monitor aircraft. P-47D-2-RE 42-8532 is at Hethel, carrying the 389th's 'C' on the fin and rudder.**

Above: **Very squashed B-24L-5-FO 44-49279 from the 389th BG's 564th BS at Fundenhall Norfolk, on 4th March 1945. After take-off for a mission to Aschaffenburg she suffered power failure, resulting in a crash-landing. A Liberator crash-landing was a very hazardous undertaking due to the wing mounted high on the fuselage and the weight of fuel, structure and engines tending to squash the fuselage into the ground. Most 'L versions of the B-24 carried a special lightweight tail turret with hand-held guns as illustrated.**

*Below:* **The beauty of the mountain scenery was undoubtedly lost on the crews of these 389th BG 'Libs' as they released their bombs whilst flying through heavy flak. Nearest the camera is B-24J-60-CF 44-10510 *You Cawn't Miss It* of the 564th BS – and she was lucky enough to survive the war.**

*Above:* **Safe back home in the USA after the conflict, B-24M-15-FO 44-50867 basking peacefully in the Arizona sun at Kingman base, awaiting the attentions of the scrapman.**

*Left:* **Six 1,000lb bombs released from B-24J-1-FO 42-50739 *Ole Buckshot* of the 389th BW, 567th BS. She was transferred to the 491st BG in May 1945.**

*Bottom left:* **566th BS B-24J-1-FO 42-50548 crash-landed just outside Hethel at East Carlton on 15th February 1945.**

*Opposite page:*

*Top:* **B-24J-5-FO 42-51474 *D-Day Patches* at rest at Hethel. She flew with the 565th BS.**

*Centre left and right:* **Two views of *Ginny Gal*, B-24H-25-FO 42-95077 from the 565th Squadron following a crash-landing in Switzerland after sustaining battle damage on 21st July 1944.**

*Bottom:* **B-24H-25-FO 42-95227 *Sibonnette* of the 564th BS undergoing maintenance at Hethel prior to having her garish beast-nose painted on – see the nose art portfolio. She flew with the 564th until crash-landing at Leconfield, Yorkshire on 4th February 1945.**

D-DAY
Patches

295077

## 445th BOMBARDMENT GROUP (H)

The 445th moved to the UK in November 1943 and took up residence at Tibenham, Norfolk, from where it flew its first mission on 13th December 1943. During its combat career the 445th completed 282 missions, dropping 16,732 tons of bombs, claiming 89 enemy aircraft destroyed with 31 probables and 37 damaged. It lost 133 of its Liberators in this period, the 445th holding the tragic record of sustaining the highest loss rate on a single mission – no less than 25 'Libs' were lost on 27th September 1944. The 445th was awarded a Distinguished Unit Citation for the Gotha raid of 24th February 1944.

**Group Markings**
White disc on upper surface of olive drab aircraft, black on silver, with a capital 'F' within the disc. White disc on vertical tail, outer surfaces with dark blue capital 'F', until May 1944 when outer tail surfaces were painted black with white horizontal band.

Squadron codes were grey on olive drab and black on silver aircraft. Many aircraft carried their call letter in deep yellow on the fuselage aft of the codes. Quite a few Liberators in this group carried yellow squadron code letters also. Squadron codes were:

| | |
|---|---|
| 700th Squadron | 'IS -' |
| 701st Squadron | 'MK -' |
| 702nd Squadron | 'WV -' |
| 703rd Squadron | 'RN -' |

From April 1944 with the introduction of the all-black tail with horizontal white stripe, call-letters were adorned as follows:

| | |
|---|---|
| 700th Squadron | '+' |
| 701st Squadron | 'bar' above |
| 702nd Squadron | 'bar' below |
| 703rd Squadron | no sign |

*Opposite page, top:* **The 701st Squadron's *Grim Reaper*, B-24J-100-CO 42-100404. She had a long career with the 445th BG and saw out the war.**

*Below, centre:* **One of the 445th BG's original Liberators in flight, B-24H-1-FO 42-7563 'P+' *Hell's Warrior*. The early batch of 'H version Liberators featured very large national insignia on the fuselage, the white of which was toned down to make it less conspicuous. Of interest is the number '9' on port outer engine cowling, while the outer starboard engine carried the number '3'. These were reference points for the top turret gunner when crew members were calling out attacking enemy fighters and using the clock system of sighting. *Hell's Warrior* was later transferred to the 492nd BG (second organisation).**

*Left:* **B-24H-1-FO 42-7586 'Q+' after the pilots pulled off a very successful crash-landing having been shot up by fighters eight miles east of Fürstenau. She came to rest on her belly on the Karwar Marshes, near Neuruppin, 25 miles north west of Berlin on 6th March 1944. It was better, if possible, to crash-land a 'Lib' with its undercarriage down as this gave the crew a better chance of walking away from the wreck. Note circle 'B' on upper wing – a legacy of previous service with 93rd BG.**

*Above, centre:* **B-24H-1-FO 42-7513 of the 445th's 702nd BS at Dübendorf, Switzerland on 18th March 1944. With one engine losing oil and another with propeller feathered she managed to limp into the field after a mission to Friedrichshafen, her landing gear severing the high voltage lead cable to the Swiss Federal Railways.**

*Right:* **Displaying 27 mission symbols on her flight-deck armour plate *Conquest Cavalier* cruises over scattered cloud in the Spring of 1944. B-24H-1-CF 41-29126 was one of the 445th's original aircraft and flew with the 701st BS.**

*Top:* ***Fearless Fosdick*** **after having pulled-off a very successful crash-landing in a cornfield at Westley Waterless, near Newmarket, Cambridgeshire, on 1st August 1944 after a mission to Nanteuil, France. The flight crew have saved the aircraft from extensive damage by lowering the wheels, always the wisest option in a 'Lib' if at all possible.** ***Fearless Fosdick*** **was B-24H-15-CF 41-29604 'WV-Y' from the 445th's 702nd BS.**

*Above, centre:* ***Blasted Event*** **of the 700th BS has not had an accident – her tail-down posture is probably due to careless unloading. B-24H-15-CF 41-29487 was engaged on a fuel trucking mission to France in aid of Patton's fuel-thirsty army.**

*Left:* **A veteran 445th 'Lib' which survived hostilities was B-24H-20-FO 42-94921** ***Tahelenback*** **which flew with both the 701st and 703rd.**

*Above:* **A 703rd BS B-24H-20-FO (serial unknown) after an extensive re-spray prior to return to USA.**

*Below, centre left:* **One of the 445th's original B-24H-1-FOs, 42-7622 *Ann* of the 701st BS.**

*Below, centre right:* **B-24H-1-FO 42-7571 of the 700th BS, *Lillian Ann II,* at ease on her hardstand. She was lost when she crashed at Dübendorf, Switzerland on 11th July 1944.**

*Bottom left:* **B-24J-95-CO 42-100343 of the 703rd BS, 445th BG, came to grief when port main landing gear collapsed on touching down on 16th September 1944 at Tibenham.**

*Bottom right:* **B-24J-95-CO 42-100353 of the 445th BG came to grief when it crash-landed in a field at Fressingfield, Suffolk, after a Berlin mission on 8th March 1944.**

*Above:* ***Ole King Cole*** **'IS-Q+', gleaming new B-24J-1-FO 42-50565 poses proudly on its hardstand at Tibenham. This 'Lib' features the new 'High Hat' top turret which gave more headroom for the gunner and allowed for the fitting of the later gun sights. It has yet to be fitted with the navigator's side bubble window.**

*Left:* **B-24H-25-DT 42-51105** ***Sweetest Rose of Texas*** **of the 701st BS, 445th BG.**

*Left, third down:* **Target-bound over scattered cloud,** ***Stormy*** **(B-24J-1-FO 42-50574) of the 702nd BS, leads** ***Hitler's Hearse*** **of the 703rd BS, 445th BG.**

*Bottom left:* **'WV-P', B-24J-1-DT 42-51252, from the 702nd BS, having just rolled up its bomb doors prior to bomb release.**

*Opposite page:*

*Top:* **After suffering a mid-air collision on the mission to Mainz on 9th September 1944, B-24H-30-FO 42-95308 from the 702nd BS, 445th BG, lost approximately 4ft off its left wing and so headed for the emergency field at Woodbridge, Suffolk, where it employed the standard emergency braking system – parachutes lashed to the waist-gun mounts and opened whilst rolling down the runway.**

*Bottom:* **Peacefully basking in the sun at Tibenham between missions is B-24J-1-FO 42-50732 from the 700th BS – another fortunate 'Lib' that got through the war.**

295308
C
VC

D+
IS D+

### 453rd BOMBARDMENT GROUP (H)

The 453rd Bomb Group arrived at its base at Old Buckenham on 22nd December 1943 and flew its first mission on 5th February 1944. The 453rd Bomb Group completed 259 missions with one of its squadrons completing 82 consecutive missions without losing an aircraft – a record. A total of 15,804 tons of ordnance was released upon the enemy with claims for 42 enemy aircraft destroyed, 12 probables and 19 damaged. The 453rd lost 58 Liberators. Its last mission was flown on 25th April 1945.

**Group Markings**

These comprised a disc containing a capital letter 'J' on the top surface of the starboard wing (white on olive drab aircraft, black on silver). A white disc with a dark blue 'J' superimposed, was painted on the vertical tail surfaces until May 1944 when tails were painted black with a diagonal white band.

The 453rd adopted squadron colours and painted their propeller spinners thus:

732nd Squadron – white
733rd Squadron – blue
734th Squadron – red
735th squadron – yellow

However, a certain amount of confusion can arise when trying to identify the squadron by its spinner colour due to aircraft transferring to a different squadron and not having their spinners repainted, which was a common practise.

Squadron code letters were painted grey on olive drab, black on silver, as follows:

| | |
|---|---|
| 732nd Squadron | 'E3 -' |
| 733rd Squadron | 'F8 -' |
| 734th Squadron | 'E8 - |
| 735th Squadron | 'H6 -' |

Many of the 453rd aircraft didn't display their squadron code letters later in the war. From April 1944 with the introduction of the all-black tail with diagonal white stripe, call-letters were adorned as follows:

| | |
|---|---|
| 732nd Squadron | no sign |
| 733rd Squadron | '+' after |
| 734th Squadron | 'bar' after |
| 735th Squadron | 'bar' below |

*Below:* **The 453rd BG heads out on another strike. B-24H-10-FO 42-52277 is nearest the camera. The latter flew with the 733rd BS and went down over Holland on a mission to Handorf on 23rd March 1944.**

*Above and centre right:* **Two views of *The Golden Gaboon*, B-24H-5-DT 41-28645, at the start and finish of her combat career. She crash-landed and burned at Old Buckenham on 30th May 1944 after the Oldenburg mission and shortly after acquiring her new black and white tail markings.**

*Below:* **B-24H-10-CF 42-64478 *Cabin in the Sky* from the 453rd's 735th BS. She had received a new port rudder which had not had the final third of the white disc painted on. *Cabin in the Sky* was lost on 27th March 1944 when she received a direct flak hit during the mission to Pau-Point Long airfield.**

*Above:* **Seen at Dübendorf, Switzerland, after the mission to Manheim on 25th April 1944. B-24H-10-CF 42-64496 *Borsuk's Bitch* from the 453rd's 735th BS experienced mechanical problems which made it impossible for her to return to England.**

*Left:* **With the most hazardous part of the mission behind her, B-24H-20-FO 42-94805 *Foil Proof* of the 735th BS crosses the continental coastline and heads for Old Buckenham – she managed this no less than 111 times in her long combat career.**

*Bottom:* **Previously operated by the 491st BG, B-24J-140-CO 42-110149 *Mary Harriet* in repose on her hardstand. She flew with the 453rd BG's 733rd Squadron and returned to the USA at the war's end. Note the decidedly patched-up appearance with replacement rudders, engine cowlings, field modified waist-gun windows and even a new Emerson nose turret in place of her original Motor Products version.**

*Opposite page:*

*Top:* **B-24H-5-DT 41-28654 *Spare Parts* drones on through a contrail-filled sky early in 1944. She was badly damaged on the mission to Berlin on 6th March 1944.**

*Bottom:* **Three B-24Hs from the 732nd BS in tight formation. B-24H-10-FO 42-52201 *Battle Package* is in the lead: she was lost on the Munich mission on 11th July 1944. Nearest the camera is B-24H-10-CF 42-64469 *El Flako*, which was lost on its 78th mission, when it broke in half after receiving a direct flak hit. In the background is *Ken-O-Kay*, B-24H-10-FO 42-52302, which was lost on the mission to Fürth on 25th February 1944.**

251301
T+

251114
J+

*Opposite page top:* **B-24J-5-DT 42-51301 *Ruth Marie* of the 733rd Squadron. She does not carry squadron code letters, but the '+' sign after the call-letter on the fin denotes it as a 733rd machine, although the assigned placing for the '+' was above the letter – not easy on the diagonal white stripe. Note also the serial painted on the inside of the port fin.**

*Opposite page bottom:* **Pleasing view of three 733rd Squadron B-24s outward bound on a mission. The nearest ship is *Whiskey Jingles*, B-24H-25-DT 42-51114.**

*This page top:* **A Liberator which happily survived the war was the 453rd BG's *Ohio Silver* from the 732nd BS, squatting on her hardstand with the sun reflecting off the life-sized white horse on her side. She was B-24H-25-FO 42-95206 which completed over 100 missions.**

*This page bottom:* **B-24H-20-DT 42-51102 *Jug Head* undergoing engine maintenance at Old Buckenham. She crashed on landing when port main landing gear gave out on 29th January 1945.**

*Top:* **Formation monitor for the 453rd BG was veteran Republic P-47C-5-RE Thunderbolt 41-6630, complete with the Group's diagonal stripe across the black fin and rudder. An RAF Avro Lancaster is in the background.**

*Above:* **A Christmas party for local children was held at Old Buckenham on Christmas Eve 1944. The British children donated toys and the Americans food for a number of children in France and a Liberator was selected to fly the goods over to Paris. B-24J-130-CO 42-110078 'H6-P' had her nose specially painted for the occasion and was christened *Liberty Run*. This Liberator survived the war with 100 missions to her credit.**

*From the top:* **Four views of the 389th BG's formation assembly ship resplendent in its silver finish with bright green and yellow stripes. Known as *The Green Dragon* during her role with the Hethel-based groups, she originally operated with the 93rd BG where she carried the name *Jo-Jo's Special Delivery*. A B-24D-1-CO (41-23683), note her needle-bladed propellers, an outward visual characteristic of the very early 'Ds. Most assembly ships discarded defensive armament but twin guns are evident in the top and rear turrets. *The Green Dragon* was salvaged after crash-landing at Manston, Kent on 25th July 1944.**

*Top:* **Veteran B-24D-20-CO 41-24215, which was formerly *Lucky Gordon* of the 93rd BG, was acquired by the 445th Bomb Group and became its assembly ship, resplendent in orange and black stripes.**

*Centre and left:* **With the sun reflecting from her bright yellow squares, *Wham Bam* squats on its hardstand at Old Buckenham and, from above, in her element. *Wham Bam* was B-24D-1-CO 41-23738 and before becoming the assembly ship with the 453rd BG she flew operationally with the 93rd BG.**

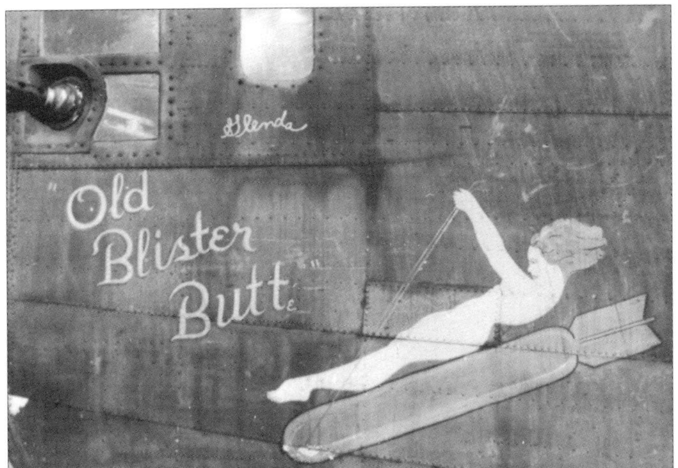

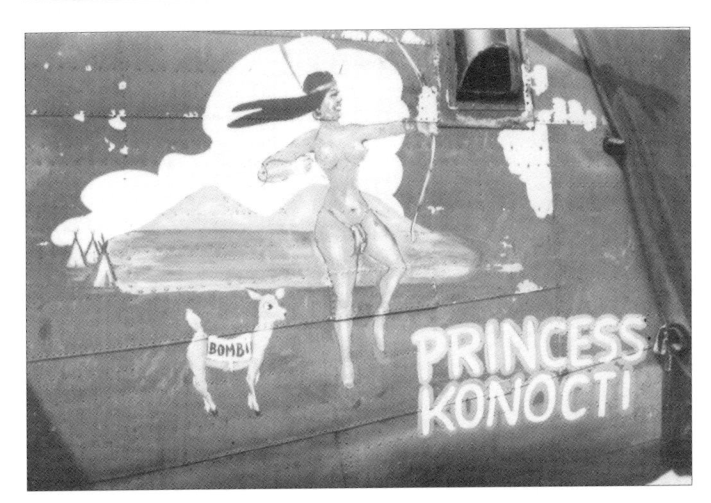

**389th BOMBARDMENT GROUP:**

**B-24D-95-CO 42-72866 *Jackass Male*.**

**B-24D-95-CO 42-40776 *Old Blister Butt* from the 564th BS.**

**Front and rear (bottom right) of B-24J-80-CO 42-100190 'J+' *Princess Konocti* of the 566th BS. Along with a somewhat raunchy Indian squaw, was a small deer, named *Bombi*.**

***Touch of Texas* rests on her hardstand at Hethel. B-24D-95-CO 42-40751 flew with both the 566th and 567th Squadrons, and is illustrated after completing 28 missions (including the slanting Ploesti bomb tally) and survived until 13th February 1944 when she was written off after nose wheel failure.**

**B-24D-165-CO 42-72871 *Miss Liberty* of the 567th Squadron. She was eventually transferred to the 492nd BG (2nd organisation).**

**389th BOMBARDMENT GROUP:**

**B-24D-165-CO 42-72876 *Lucky Tiger* of the 566th BS.**

**B-24J-130-CO 42-110084 *Don't Cry Baby* of the 565th BS.**

**B-24J-105-CO 42-109792 *Wicked Widget III* of the 567th BS.**

***Mistah Chick* of the 567th BS, B-24J-75-CO 42-100146.**

**B-24D-95-CO 42-40746 *Ole Irish* of the 564th BS.**

**B-24J-105-CO 42-109794 *Nuff Sed* of the 565th Squadron, was lost on 21st June 1944.**

**389th BOMBARDMENT GROUP:**

**B-24H-15-DT 41-28824 *Sack Warmer* flew with the 566th BS. The nose-art has been partially obscured by the appliqué armour plate.**

**B-24D-15-CF 42-63959 *Southern Queen* of the 566th BS. Note that 'Southern' has been painted out and a question mark applied.**

**B-24J-5-FO 42-51451 *The Carrier Pigeon* of the 564th BS.**

**B-24D-15-CF 42-63956 *Old Glory* 'EE-X' of the 565th BS.**

**B-24J-85-CO 42-100281 *Naughty Norma* of the 566th BS.**

**B-24H-30-DT 42-51193 *Lucky Lady Betty II* of the 565th BS crashed in Yorkshire on 31st January 1945.**

**389th BOMBARDMENT GROUP:**

**B-24J-40-CF 42-50452 *Earthquake McGoon* of the 566th BS. It crashed at Carleton Rode, Norfolk, on 21st November 1944.**

**B-24J-1-FO 42-50551 *Delectable Doris* flew with the 566th BS she was lost to flak on the Magdeburg mission on 3rd February 1945.**

**B-24J-65-CF 44-10579 *Pugnacious Princess Pat* of the 566th BS – lost on 26th November 1944.**

**B-24J-5-fo 42-51474 *D-Day Patches* of the 565th BS – written off after nose wheel collapse on 10th May 1945.**

**B-24J-1-FO 42-50558 'RR-F+' *Miss America* of the 566th BS – lost on Dortmund mission on 28th January 1945.**

**B-24J-1-FO 42-50739 *Ole Buckshot* flew with the 567th BS before transferring to 491st BG in May 1945.**

**389th BOMBARDMENT GROUP:**

**Most Bomb Groups in the 2nd Air Division had garishly painted 'beast nose' 'Libs' on strength and the 389th was no exception. B-24H-25-FO 42-95227, *Sibonnette* flew in the 564th BS.**

**445th BOMBARDMENT GROUP:**

**B-24H-1-CF 41-29138 *Boys Howdy* of the 445th's 700th BS after flying its 29th mission.**

**B-24H-1-FO 42-7541 *Sweatin it Out* of the 700th BS. She survived until 11th November 1944 when she was declared war-weary.**

**445th BOMBARDMENT GROUP:**

**B-24J-1-FO 42-50592 *Lady Marian*, 701st BS, survived the war.**

**B-24H-20-FO 42-94828 *You're Safe at Home* of the 703rd BS. Transferred to the 448th in February 1945.**

**B-24H-20-FO 42-94921 *Tahelenbak* of the 701st BS.**

**B-24H-1-FO 42-7619 *Bunnie* of the 700th BS crashed on take-off for its 108th mission on 24th February 1945.**

**B-24H-20-FO 42-94863 *Ole Baldy* of the 701st BS. It was lost on 27th September 1944 on a mission to Kassel.**

**B-24H-20-FO 42-95015 *Patches* of the 700th BS, also survived the war.**

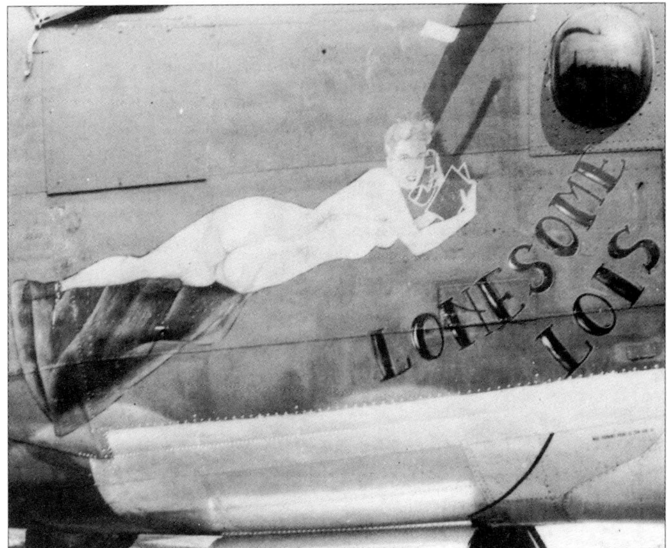


**445th BOMBARDMENT GROUP:**

**B-24H *Clay Pidgeon* served with the 445th BG.**

**A sad ending for *Ole King Cole* after a non-operational flight on the 27th March 1945. B-24J-1-FO 42-50565 'IS-Q+', *Ole King Cole* flew with the 700th BS.**

**B-24H-20-FO of the 703rd BS (serial unknown) with navigator's 'eye, 'shark's mouth' and a winged badge.**

**B-24J-5-FO 42-51532 *Hot Rock* of the 703rd BS was lost on a Kassel mission, 27th September 1944.**

***Lonesome Lois*, Ford-built B-24H-20-FO 42-95020 of the 701st BS. She survived the war, even after a crash-landing at Beccles, Suffolk on 13th July 1944, when a nose wheel collapse caused damage to the underside.**

"VAMPIN'
VERA"

"CORKY"
BURGUNDY BOMBERS
MISS
ELLAMAE
656

PLUCKY LUCKY

SILENT
YOKUM

HARD T GET

**453rd BOMBARDMENT GROUP:**

*Opposite page:*

**B-24H-10-CF 41-29301 *Vampin' Vera* operated with the 732nd BS.**

**B-24H-20-FO 42-94820 *Plucky Lucky* operated with the 735th BS, but was originally with the 489th BG.**

**B-24H-10-FO 42-52299 *Hard T'Get* of the 732nd BS went down in English Channel on 1st August 1944.**

**B-24H-10-FO 42-52234 *Corky* flew with 733rd BS. Note the 'sub-title' *Burgundy Bombers*.**

**B-24J-5-FO 42-50898 *Silent Yokum* flew with the 735th BS. It crashed on take-off on 27th December 1944.**

*This page:*

***Crows Nest*, B-24H-30-FO 42-95303 from the 734th BS, went to the 93rd BG late in the war.**

**Double meaning in the naming of B-24J-65-CF 44-10575 *Becoming Back*. She flew with both the 734th and 735th Bomb Squadrons and was eventually transferred to the 491st BS.**

**B-24J-150-CO 44-40173 *Our Baby* was a 453rd BG machine which survived the war.**

**B-24H-25-FO 42-95206 *Ohio Silver*, of the 732nd BS completed over 100 missions.**

**B-24H-25-DT 42-51105 *Sweetest Rose of Texas* of the 701st BS.**

**733rd BS B-24H-25-DT 42-51114 *Whiskey Jingles*.**

**453rd BOMBARDMENT GROUP:**

**B-24H-25-FO 42-95102 *Spirit of Notre Dame* proudly displaying her mission scoreboard. She flew with the 734th Squadron before transferring to the 448th BG, and is known to have flown at least 119 missions.**

**B-24H-15-DT 41-28938 *Pay Day* flew with the 732nd BS but was originally a 491st BG aircraft.**

**B-24H-10-CF 42-64473 *Yuvadit* carried the name *Lovers' Lane* on port side of nose. She flew with the 735th BS and survived the war.**

**B-24J-130-CO 42-110078 *Liberty Run* used for the Old Buckenham Christmas present run to Paris on 24th December 1944.**

**B-24J-10-FO 42-51707 *Dorothy*. Note stains from two vents and the nose wheel circle graticule.**

Chapter Three

# 14th Combat Bomb Wing

*Above:* **B-24Ds of the 44th BG taxi out through the mud of the newly-completed Shipdham airfield on their way to a practise mission .**

## 44th BOMBARDMENT GROUP (H)
***The Flying Eightballs***

The first of the 14th CBW's bomb groups to arrive in the United Kingdom was the veteran 44th Group – *The Flying Eightballs*. Their British service commenced on September 1942 at Cheddington, Herts, moving within a very short time to Shipdham in Norfolk, starting on 10th October 1942. The flight and ground crews of the *Flying Eightballs* together with the 93rd Bombardment Group (BG) over at Alconbury, Huntingdonshire, were the first to introduce the Liberator to the enemy and flew their first combat mission on 7th November 1942 about four weeks after the 93rd's initial raid. This first mission was a diversionary sweep over the Low Countries. The 44th then went on to complete a total of 343 missions including 18 on detachments to North Africa.

The *Eightballs* were on two occasions awarded Distinguished Unit Citations, for the Kiel mission on the 14th May and for the low level mission against the Ploesti oil fields on the 1st August 1943. The Group Commander at the time, Colonel Leon W Johnson was awarded the Congressional Medal of Honor for his leadership on the Ploesti attack.

During the 44th's long combat career their B-24s dropped 18,980 tons of bombs. They lost 192 Liberators and claimed 330 enemy aircraft destroyed, 74 probables and 69 damaged.

For nearly the first year of their combat career the *Eightballs* flew the B-24D version of the Liberator and this model was taken out to North Africa for their two detachments; the first starting on 28th June 1943 when the lush pastures of Norfolk were forsaken for the heat and dust of Benina Main in Libya where they stayed until 25th August. The 44th returned to Shipdham for a little over three weeks before setting off for Africa once again this time to Oudna No.1 airfield in Tunisia from September 19th until October 4th.

On return from their first Mediterranean adventure the group started receiving, as new replacement aircraft, B-24H and 'J models with the new nose turrets and, over the months, these improved versions gradually took the place of the old 'Ds although some of them soldiered on well into 1944. The 44th flew its final mission on 25th April 1945.

**Group Markings**

During the first year of its operational career the 44th BG did not carry any distinguishing group markings on its wing or tail surfaces and the vertical tails were plain olive drab apart from the serial number and the aircraft's individual call-letter, both in deep yellow.

During the Group's detachment to North Africa many of its B-24s had an RAF-style fin flash of red white and blue applied to the tail as they flew under RAF command during this period.

Upon return to England in September 1943 the group applied the new 2nd Air Division (AD) markings to its aircraft – a white disc on the upper starboard wing upon which an insignia blue capital 'A' was incorporated. A white disc with a blue capital 'A' was also applied to the vertical tail surfaces until May 1944. Most of the 44th's early deliveries, and a few of its later ones, carried a *Flying Eightball* insignia on the port sides of their noses.

Fuselage code letter groupings applied from March 1944 were grey on olive drab aircraft, and in black on silver (or 'natural metal') machines:

| | |
|---|---|
| 66th Squadron | 'QK-' |
| 67th Squadron | 'NB-' |
| 68th Squadron | 'WQ-' |
| 506th Squadron | 'GJ-' |

From April/May 1944 vertical tails were white or silver with a black vertical band. As with other Liberators within the 2nd AD, 'bars' and '+' signs were applied to the aircraft call-letters as follows:

| | |
|---|---|
| 66th Squadron | '+' after |
| 67th Squadron | 'bar' below |
| 68th Squadron | no sign |
| 506th Squadron | 'bar' above |

*Above:* **The *Eightballs* practice formation flying over Wicklewood, Norfolk, just a few miles from their base at Shipdham. All are B-24D-5-COs, 'S' is 41-23774 *Hitler's Nightmare*, 'X' is 41-23816 *Black Jack* and 'L' is 41-23817 *Suzy Q*.**

*Left:* ***Timb-a-a-ah!* about to take-off in North Africa. She was B-24D-75-CO 42-40606. After surviving the low level Ploesti mission she was shot down by fighters on the Foggia mission on 16th August 1943.**

*Top:* **Lt James O'Brien's *Rugged Buggy*, B-24D-5-CO 41-23819 of the 68th BS, 44th BG was lost over Kiel on the 14th May 1943.**

*Above, centre:* ***Avenger II*, B-24D-30-CO 42-40130 of the 68th BS was interned in Spain after a raid on Bordeaux, France on 17th May 1943.**

*Right:* **B-24D-15-CF 42-63962 from the 67th BS, 44th BG could not make its mind up what to call itself. Here it is called *Prince* but was at sometime called *Princ-ass* and finally *Princess*. It was interned in Sweden, bearing that name, after force-landing there during a mission to Pölitz on 29th May 1944.**

*Left:* ***The Impatient Virgin*****, B-24H-5-CF 41-29231 from the 67th BS, 44th BG.**

*Centre left:* **B-24D-1-CO 41-23699** ***Lemon Drop*** **of the 68th BS over the desert during the 44th's second deployment to the Middle East in September 1943. Note the RAF-style fin flashes.** ***Lemon Drop*** **later became the 44th Bomb Group's assembly aircraft.**

*Bottom:* **The 44th BG's** ***Princess Charlotte*****, B-24D-5-CO 41-23769 of the 68th BS.**

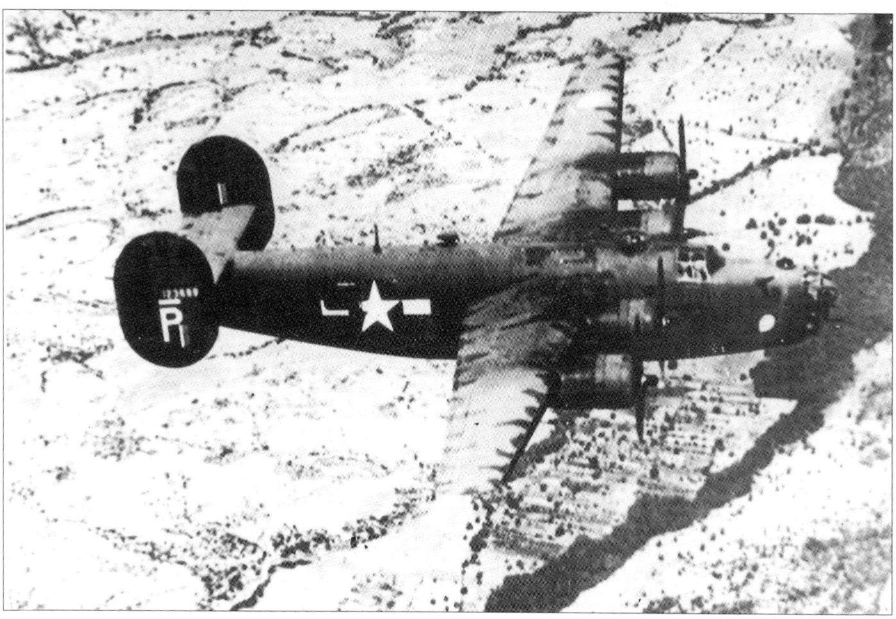


*Opposite page:*

*Top:* ***Victory Ship*** **(B-24D-5-CO 41-23813) forms a backdrop to a ceremony at Shipdham on 22nd November 1943 for General Johnson's award of the Medal of Honor from General Devers. The censor has deleted the** ***Flying Eightball*** **insignia on the nose.**

*Bottom:* **One of those badly damaged on the mission to destroy an aircraft repair depot at Oslo, Norway, on 18th November 1943 was B-24H-1-CF 41-29161 of the 67th BS, 44th BG, flown by Lt R C Griffith. On the return to Shipdham, Lt Griffith ordered seven members of the crew to bale out leaving himself, co-pilot Lt L W Grone and badly wounded gunner, Sgt W T Kuban, aboard. A spectacular crash-landing was made with no further injuries being sustained.**

A

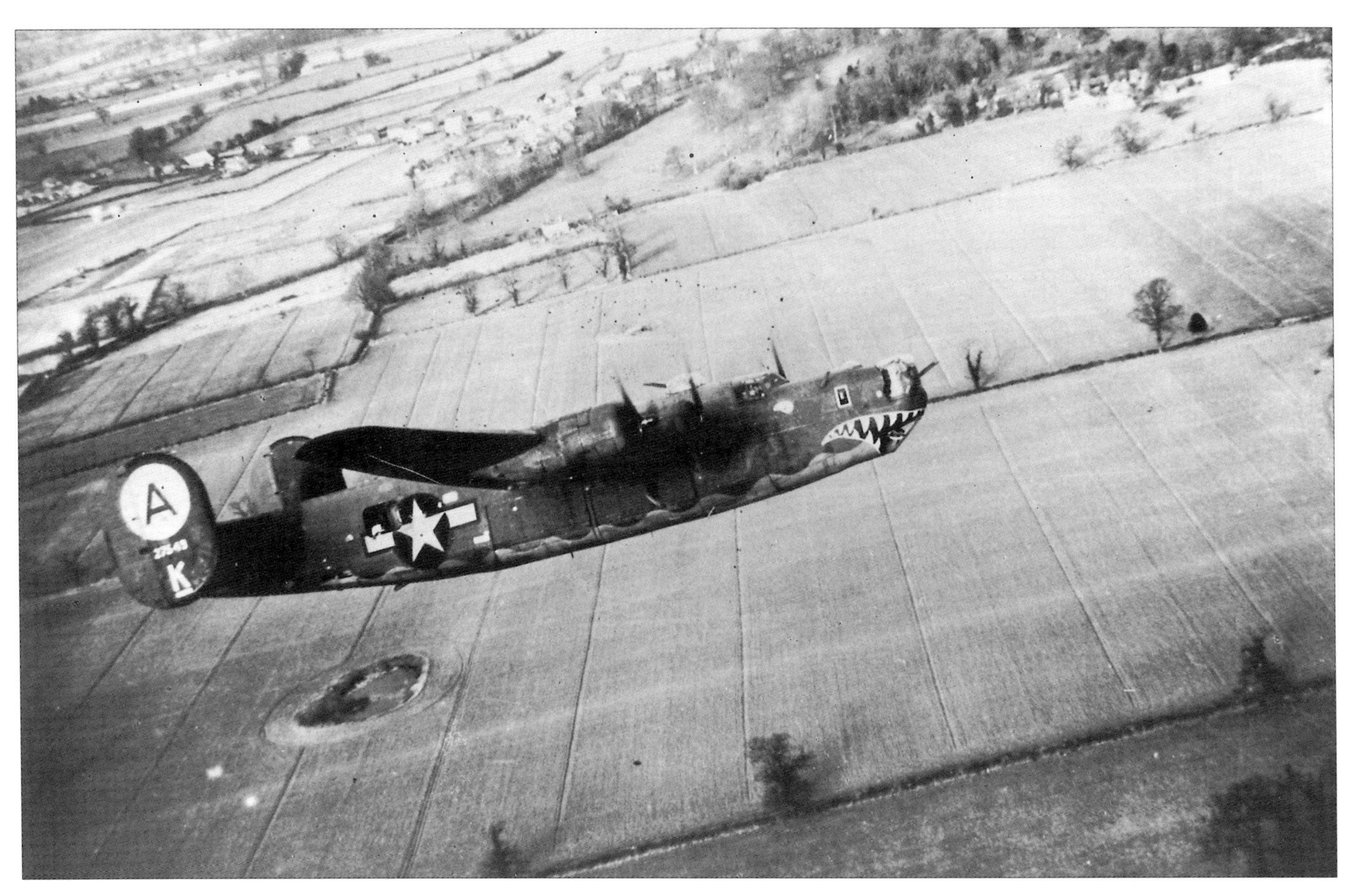


*Above:* **Shark-mouth decorated B-24H-1-FO 42-7549 assigned to 67th BS (note the 'bar' below the call-letter on the fin) banks low over the Norfolk countryside near the 44th BG's base at Shipdham.**

*Below:* **Groundcrews wishing luck on their charges as the 44th taxies around the perimeter track prior to take-off. The 'Lib's' wingspan can be appreciated in this view.**

**Five of the eight 44th BG B-24s lost on the 18th March 1944 mission to Friedrichshafen sought sanctuary in Switzerland.** *Top left:* **68th BS B-24J-70-CO 42-100112 piloted by Lt Hollis R Nichols crashed near Dietschwil. The other four force-landed at Dübendorf;** *Top right:* **B-24J-100-CO 42-100400 of the 506th BS, piloted by Lt Robert R Lucas;** *Above, second down:* **B-24H-1-FO 42-7618 of the 66th BS, piloted Lt George D Telford;** *Above, third down:* **B-24H-15-CF 41-29431 of the 506th BS, piloted by 2/Lt Winston C Irwin and** *Bottom right:* **B-24J-105-CO 42-109800 from 68th BS, piloted by 2/Lt Eugene N Dyer.**

*Top:* **B-24J-90-CO 42-100330 from the 67th BS, 44th BG at Dübendorf, Switzerland, after force-landing there on 13th April 1944 during a mission to Lechfeld airfield. The pilot was Lt Rockford C Griffith.**

*Left:* ***Forky II*** **rests in the sun at Shipdham. A B-24D-35-CO (42-40182) of the 66th BS, she was lost on the Ploesti mission on 1st August 1943 crashing into a cornfield and exploding on leaving target.**

*Below:* **The later versions of the B-24D were equipped with a ball-turret. B-24D-160-CO 42-72857 from the 506th BS was lost on 1st October 1943 during the mission to Wiener Neustadt, Austria.**

*Top:* **A Christmas greeting from Shipdham 1943 – with the girl on the nose of *Southern Comfort* completely out of her element in the Norfolk snow. She was B-24H-1-FO (42-7522) from the 506th BS. *Southern Comfort* was lost on 11th April 1944 when the starboard bomb bay door failed to open. A fragmentation bomb hit the closed door setting the aircraft on fire and causing it to break in two.**

*Bottom:* **Two Liberators from the 44th BG's 68th BS. The nearest aircraft, B-24H-25-FO 42-95260 *Lily Marlene*, crashed on take-off at Shipdham in December 1944.**

*Left:* **Several freshly painted over flak patches visible on the rear fuselage of B-24D-5-CO 41-23811 *Fascinatin Witch* from the 66th BS as she taxies past the camera. The *Witch* was lost on the 1st October 1943 mission to Wiener Neustadt, Austria.**

*Centre left:* **B-24H-25-CF 42-50381 from the 68th BS, 44th BG was lost on 18th October 1944 during a mission to Leverkusen.**

*Bottom:* ***My Gal Sal*, 44th BG B-24J-1-FO 42-50626 from the 506th BS being cannibalised at Shipdham after crash-landing there on 30th August 1944.**

*Opposite page:*

*Top:* **B-24J-60-CF 44-10548 from the 66th BS, 44th BG. Note the radio counter-measures (RCM) aerials on the nose and under the forward fuselage. The '+' sign after the call-letter on 66th aircraft could not be accommodated within the vertical black band and was applied, in black, to the rudder.**

*Centre:* **The 44th BG's *Sweat Box* had its port undercarriage collapse when landing at Shipdham on 5th November 1944. A B-24J-145-CO (44-40071) of the 66th BS, *Sweat Box* originally flew with the 492nd.**

*Bottom:* ***Southern Comfort III* taxies out from its hardstand at Shipdham. B-24J-5-FO (42-50896), from the 506th BS, was shot down by ground fire during the 44th BG's low level supply mission to Wesel in support of the Rhine crossing on the 24th March 1945. The pilot on that occasion was Lt Leonard J Crandell.**

410548
Q
QK

SOUTHERN
COMFORT
III

*Left:* **A new B-24M-5-FO (44-50578) gets airborne from Shipdham early Spring 1945. She was transferred to the 44th from the 491st BG.**

*Centre left and bottom:* **Two contrasting photos taken before the 44th BG's final mission to Tirstrup, Denmark on 12th April 1945. *Glory Bee*, battle scarred and camouflaged veteran B-24H-15-FO 42-52616, from the 66th BS, tucks up its wheels on take-off for its 98th mission, and a pathfinder B-24L of the 506th BS taxies from its hardstand on the way to its 13th mission.**

*Photographs on the opposite page:*

*Top:* **Liberators of the 44th BG's 68th BS en route to Saarbrücken. The nearest aircraft, B-24H-30-CF 42-50427 *Puritanical Bitch*, crashed at Shipdham on 22nd March 1945.**

*Bottom:* **The 68th Squadron on the low level supply drop to airborne troops in Holland. 'WQ-E' is B-24H-20-DT 42-51101 *Corky*, whilst the nearest aircraft, 'WQ-V', is B-24H-30-CF 42-50427 *Puritanical Bitch*, also seen in the illustration above. *Corky* was lost on 28th January 1945 on a Dortmund mission.**

A
WQ
C

GJ

## 392nd BOMBARDMENT GROUP (H)
### *The Crusaders*

The 392nd Bomb Group (BG), known as *The Crusaders* crossed the Atlantic during August 1943 and settled at Wendling, Norfolk whilst the only other Liberator Groups, the 44th, 93rd and 389th were over in North Africa. The 392nd Bomb Group was the first to be equipped with the new nose-turreted Liberators, mostly Ford-built B-24Hs but with a few 'J models also.

*The Crusaders* flew their first combat mission to Abbeville, France on the 9th September 1943 – and went on to fly 285 combat missions all told. During its combat career the 392nd won a Distinguished Unit Citation for the mission to Gotha on 24th February 1944 and its B-24s dropped a total of 17,452 tons of bombs for the loss of 184 of its Liberators. The Group's gunners claimed 144 enemy aircraft destroyed, 45 probables and 49 damaged. *The Crusaders'* last mission was staged on 25th April 1945.

**Group Markings**

White disc incorporating an insignia blue capital 'D' on the upper surface of starboard wing and on the vertical tails on olive drab aircraft and a black disc with white capital 'D' on silver machines. From late April 1944 the Group adopted a white vertical tail with black horizontal band.

Squadron code letters were grey on olive drab and black on silver, as follows:

| | |
|---|---|
| 576th Squadron | 'CI-' |
| 577th Squadron | 'DC-' |
| 578th Squadron | 'EC-' |
| 579th Squadron | 'GC-' |

'Bars' and '+' signs were applied to the aircraft call-letters as follows:

| | |
|---|---|
| 576th Squadron | no sign |
| 577th Squadron | '+' after |
| 578th Squadron | 'bar' under |
| 579th Squadron | 'bar' above |

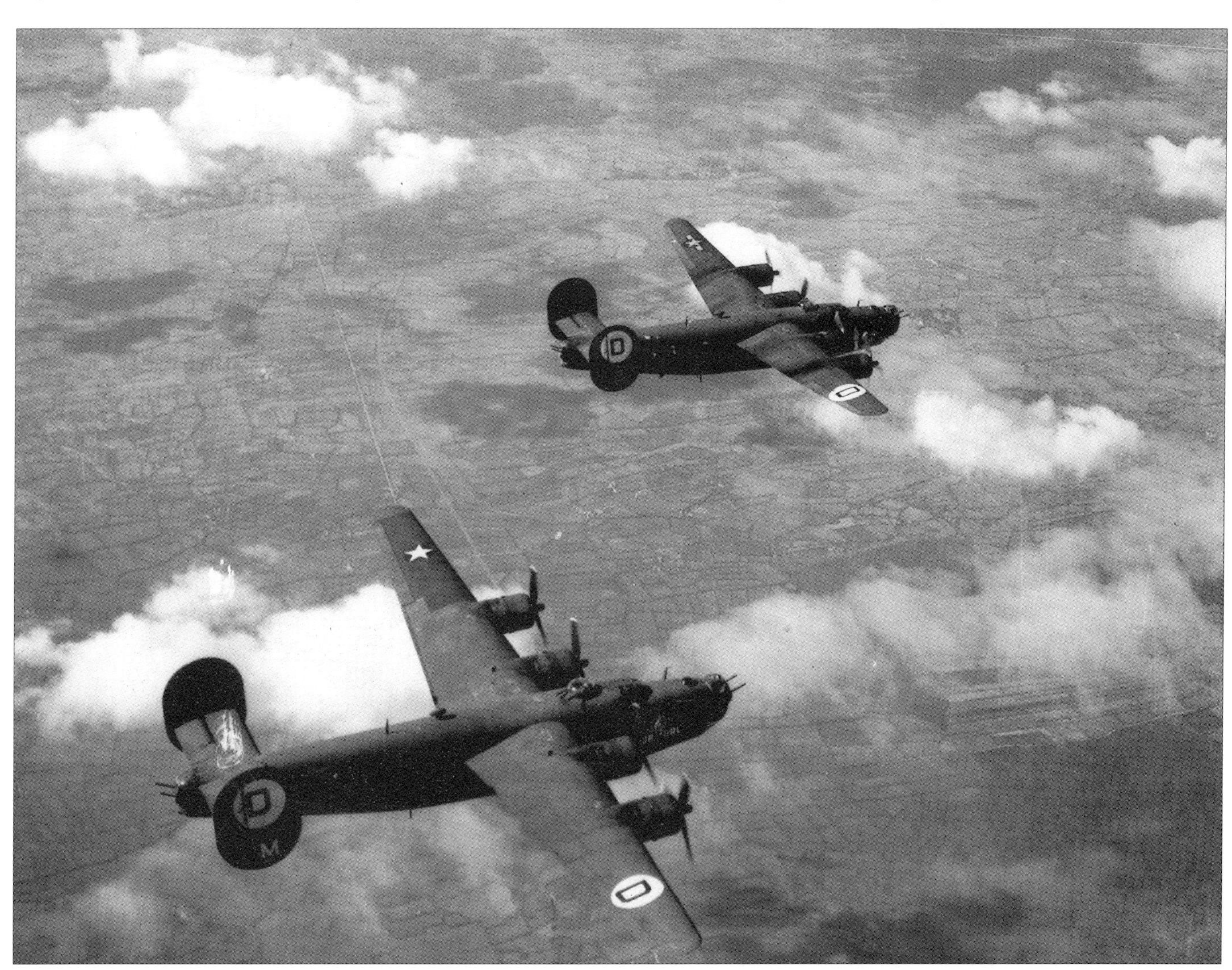

*Opposite page top:*

**Shining in the sun on their dispersal, two 68th Squadron, 44th BG, natural metal B-24s await their next mission. In the foreground is B-24J-65-CF 44-10553 'WQ-C', which crash-landed in France on 28th December 1944. 'WQ-A' in the background is B-24J-1-FO 42-50660, a pathfinder aircraft which was lost on 16th January 1945 over Alsace-Lorraine, France.**

*Opposite page, bottom:*

**Three 44th 'Libs' coming in over the north Norfolk coast in April 1945. Uppermost is the veteran B-24H-20-FO *Down De Hatch* (42-95016) showing evidence of a recently acquired additional escape hatch on top of fuselage. At lower left is B-24J-5-DT 42-51351 *Clean Sweep*, whilst nearest to the camera is brand new B-24M-10-FO 44-50748 *Big Headed Kid*. Holkham Hall with its park and lake can be seen to the lower right of the photograph.**

*This page, above:*

***Our Gal*, B-24J-90-CO 42-100308 of the 578th BS (nearest camera) and *Alfred II*, B-24H-1-FO 42-7546 of the 577th BS, formate over the English countryside. Note the old style insignia on the port wing of *Our Gal*.**

*Above:* ***Poop Deck Pappy*, B-24H-1-FO 42-7521 in 392nd BG markings, was at one time assigned to the 44th BG but was probably 'traded in' in exchange for a new B-24J as the 392nd BG much preferred the 'H version and made every effort to standardise on it.**

*Left and bottom:* **B-24H-1-FO 42-7491 *Pregnant Peg*, assigned to the 577th BS, 392nd BG, force-landed with engine trouble in a field near Ashill, Norfolk on 30th October 1943. After several weeks work lightening the aircraft by removing the front turret etc, and preparing a temporary airstrip, *Peg* was flown out successfully by Major Allen G Russell of the Ferry and Transport Service on 13th December. She was lost on a mission to Oranienburg on the 3rd March 1944.**

*Opposite page:*

*Top:* **Over the Normandy coastline returning from one of the 392nd BG's early operations are two 579th BS aircraft. *Rose of Juarez* B-24H-1-FO 42-7469 (nearest camera) and *Short Snorter* B-24J-60-CO 42-99990 which went on to complete well over 100 missions. Note the variation in shade of the olive drab paint between the aircraft manufactured at different factories.**

*Bottom:* **Two B-24s of the 392nd BG's 576th BS; the nearest aircraft is B-24H-15-CF 41-29433. Piloted by Lt A W Evans, it crashed near Swaffham, Norfolk, on 29th May 1944 when returning from a mission to Pölitz.**

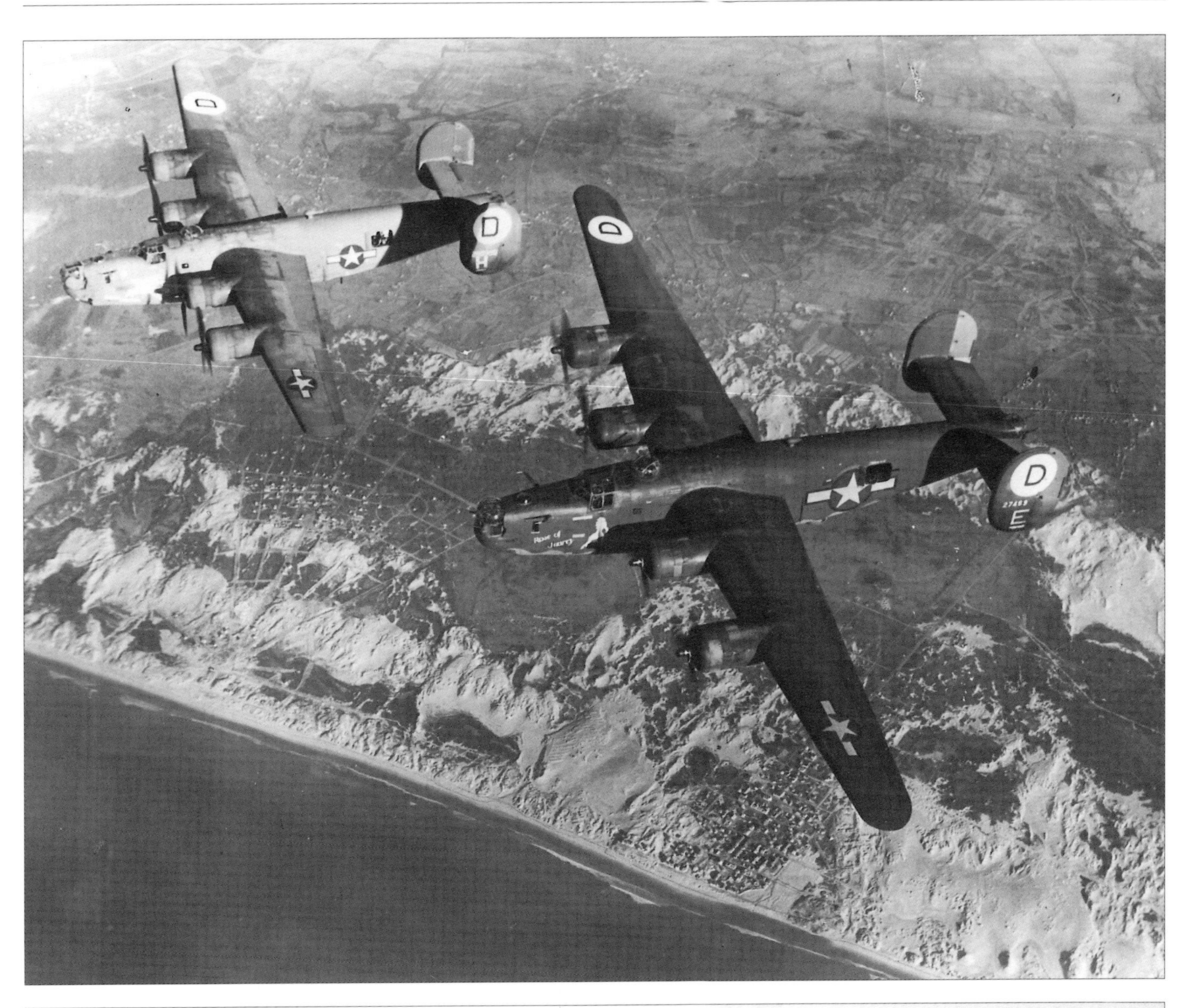
D
D
D
D
E

D
D
129433
D
CI

*Top and above, centre:* **On the 18th March 1944 the 392nd BG flew its most disastrous mission of the war. It went to Friedrichshafen and lost 15 of the 28 Liberators despatched, mainly due to heavy flak and severe fighter opposition. Two which did not return to Wendling were B-24H-10-DT 41-28692 '284' of the 576th BS, flown by Lt W J Hebron, and *Li'l Gypsy*, B-24H-1-CF 41-29127 from the 579th BS, piloted by Lt W A Kala. Both aircraft force-landed at the Swiss military airfield at Dübendorf. They were joined by another 14 B-17s and B-24s, including some Liberators from their sister unit, the 44th Bomb Group.**

*Left:* ***Rose of Juarez,* B-24H-1-FO 42-7469 of the 579th BS, 392nd BG, suffered a not uncommon occurrence with Liberators, that of nose wheel failure, when landing at Watton, Norfolk in November 1943.**

*Above:* **B-24H-1-FO 42-7466 surrounded by ground crew and vehicles at dispersal at Wendling. The 'bar' under the call-letter denotes that the 'Lib' is assigned to the 578th BS. Before long, this machine would be named *Ford's Folly* – after its manufacturers.**

*Below:* **392nd BG armourers loading *Fords' Folly* ready for a D-Day mission on 6th June 1944. The aircraft has been modified by the fitting of a navigator's scanning window which later in the war became standard on Ford-built B-24Ls and 'Ms.**

*Left and below, centre:* **These pretty snow scenes at Wendling were probably not appreciated by the ground crew working on the engines of *Alfred II*, a B-24H-1-FO (42-7546) flown with the 577th BS. On a mission to Berlin on 29th April this aircraft was badly shot-up by fighters – the crew nursed the crippled 'Lib' back to England where it was abandoned in the air. *Alfred* crashed and burned at Walcott, Norfolk.**

*Bottom:* **Ball-turret down and swivelled forward, alert for attacking fighters, *Axis Grinder* makes its way towards its objective. B-24H-1-FO 42-7495 flew with the 577th BS and she lasted out the war.**

*Right:* **Rather battered and well-used *Dragon Lady* with her bomb bay doors rolled up ready to release her lethal cargo. The metal plate covering the gap left by the removed ball turret is very evident. *Dragon Lady*, 42-94906, formerly flew with the 489th BG and was a B-24H-20-FO of the 477th BS, 392nd BG – she also survived the war.**

*Below, centre:* ***YMCA Flying Service* B-24H-10-DT 41-28700 of the 579th BS.**

*Bottom:* ***Big Ass Bird* about to touch down at Wendling. B-24H-1-FO 42-7490 flew with the 578th BS and was lost on 5th November 1943.**

*Top:* ***Hell Wagon*** **on final approach with main gear down and nose wheel about to drop. She was B-24H-1-FO 42-7492 with the 576th BS and was later transferred to the 453rd BG.**

*Centre left:* **Just prior to the end of the war, B-24H-15-FO 42-52770, *The Ruptured Duck*, looking very war-weary with replacement engine cowlings, de-icer boots removed, field modified waist windows and her nose-art overpainted for some unknown reason.**

*Bottom:* **Showing signs of wear and tear and several replacement parts 392nd BG veteran, B-24H-1-FO 42-7478 from the 578th BS. This aircraft was destroyed in a crash at West Bradenham, Norfolk on 9th October 1944.**

*Opposite page:*

*Top:* **The 392nd BG lost two B-24s on the 11th July 1944 mission to Munich, both of which force-landed at Altenrhein, Switzerland, with flak damage. One of them was B-24H-25-FO 42-95033 of the 578th BS flown by Lt G L Bridson.**

*Bottom:* **One of the early unpainted Liberators, B-24H-15-DT 41-28916 from the 392nd BG's 576th BS over the target. Note the smoke marker trails in the background.**

033

128916
O
CI
916

This page:

*Top:* ***Umbriago*****, B-24H-25-DT 42-51126 from the 392nd BG's 579th BS, flying with replacement fins and rudders, the starboard fin having been fitted 'inside-out'.**

*Bottom:* **Pathfinder from the 579th BS, 392nd BG. B-24J-5-FO 42-51459 was later named *Lady Diana II*.**

Opposite page:

*Top:* **Tail damage to B-24H-25-CF 42-50390 of the 577th BS, 392nd BG, caused during the surprise intruder attack on Wendling airfield on the evening of 20th March 1945 when eight Liberators were damaged.**

*Bottom:* **Bomb-release for three 577th BS 'Libs'. Nearest is B-24J-1-FO 42-50697 *We'll Get By*.**

250390
250390
DC

697
DC
D+

## 491st BOMBARDMENT GROUP (BG)
### *The Ringmasters*

The 491st Bomb Group, *The Ringmasters*, joined the short-lived 95th CBW of the 8th Air Force in April 1944 and was allocated the airfield at Metfield, Suffolk. Their opening combat mission was to Brétigny, France, on 2nd June 1944. When the 95th CBW was disbanded in August the 491st moved over to North Pickenham, Norfolk, to replace the 492nd Bomb Group in the 14th Combat Wing.

The 491st completed a total of 187 combat missions and obtained a Distinguished Unit Citation for the mission to Misburg on 26th November 1944. A total of 70 of its Liberators was lost whilst delivering 12,304 tons of bombs on the enemy. Nine enemy aircraft were claimed destroyed with ten probables and three damaged. The Group's final combat mission was flown on 25th April 1945.

**Group Markings**
A white disc incorporating an insignia blue 'Z' on the upper starboard wing of olive drab aircraft; alternatively a black disc and white 'Z' on the silver examples. The outer tail surfaces were painted green with a white horizontal stripe (95th CBW colours). The 491st rather belatedly started using the former 492nd BG markings of a silver tail with black diagonal stripe in the spring of 1945.

Squadron codes were grey on olive drab aircraft and black on silver machines. Some of the silver aircraft retained the grey codes and a number of the Group's B-24s had green codes to match the tails. Unit code letters were:

| | |
|---|---|
| 852nd Squadron | '3Q -' |
| 853rd Squadron | 'T8 -' |
| 854th Squadron | '6X -' |
| 855th Squadron | 'V2 -' |

'Bars' and '+' signs were applied to the aircraft call-letters as follows:

| | |
|---|---|
| 852nd Squadron | no sign |
| 853rd Squadron | 'bar' before* |
| 854th Squadron | 'bar' above* |
| 855th Squadron | '+' after |

* The 853rd also used a 'bar' below and the 854th a 'bar' after their call-letters.

*Above:* **One of the few olive drab aircraft to see service with the 491st BG was *Johnny Come Lately*, a B-24J-140-CO (42-110154) from the 855th BS, releasing 500lb bombs over the target.**

*Left:* **The 491st BG's 853rd BS 'T8-C' was called *Uninvited* and definitely uninvited was this crash-landing at Metfield on 15th June 1944. Badly holed by flak over St Cyr, France, which injured one of the crew, Lt W Stokely, the pilot, brought B-24J-145-CO 44-40124 down with no flaps or brakes and with parachutes streaming from the waist windows, without further casualties.**

*Right:* ***Little Beaver*****, B-24J-150-CO 44-40194 of the 855th BS leads a 491st BG formation.**

*Below, centre:* **The 491st BG's B-24J-150-CO 44-40165** ***Rage in Heaven*****, flew with the 852nd BS until it became the Group's second assembly ship, replacing** ***The Lil' Gramper*****. It served until it crashed on take-off in a snowstorm on 5th January 1945.**

*Bottom:* ***Grease Ball*****, B-24J-150-CO 44-40172 from the 854th BS, touches down at the 491st BG's, first base at Metfield.** ***Grease Ball*** **was lost on the Misburg mission of 26th November 1944.**

T
3X

M+
V2

*Photographs on the opposite page:*

*Top:* **Just after its arrival in England, the 491st BG was required to turn over 18 of its 'J models to other groups and received some new Ford-built B-24Hs as replacements. One of these, B-24H-25-FO 42-95218, was wrongly coded '3X' instead of the 854th BS's '6X'. '218 ended its career with the 491st some six weeks later when on 21st July 1944, piloted by 2/Lt Stanley V Scott, it force-landed with a fire in No.2 engine at Dübendorf, Switzerland, during a mission to Kempten, Germany.**

*Bottom:* **B-24J-1-NT 42-78482 of the 855th BS, 491st BG. This was a version of the Liberator built by North American at Dallas, only a few of which served with the 2nd Air Division.**

*This page top:* **A formation from the 491st BG over Norfolk en route to Eindhoven for the supply dropping mission of 18th September 1944. In the foreground is B-24J-1-FO 42-50757 from the 855th BS.**

*This page, above:* **Down at an emergency strip at Lydd, Kent, on 1st October 1944, *Bi-U-Baby*, B-24J-1-FO 42-95619 of the 491st BG, 855th BS (formerly flew with 44th BG).**

*Left:* ***Jezabelle*****, B-24J-150-CO 44-40213 flew with the 852nd BS, 491st BG.**

*Centre left:* **Radar bombing through solid cloud cover, *She Devil* B-24J-145-CO 44-40123 from the 852nd BS, 491st BG.**

*Bottom:* **A 491st BG pathfinder with radome in the ball-turret position, B-24J-10-FO 42-51691; it flew with the 855th BS.**

*Opposite page:*

*Top:* **High over the Continent, two Liberators of the 491st BG's 855th BS. Nearest is *Big Un*, B-24J-1-FO 42-50680 which was lost on 26th February 1945 when its crew baled out behind Russian lines after having engine trouble during a mission to Berlin. In the rear is B-24J-150-CO 44-40164 *Pegasus*.**

*Bottom:* **With a background of vapour trails from what, hopefully, is a high level escort of friendly fighters, B-24J-145-CO *Hare Power* (44-40117). At first glance it looks as though the bomb doors are open, but *Hare Power* is fitted with grey-painted doors from a cannibalised 'donor'. It flew with the 491st BG's 852nd BS until 26th November 1944 when it was shot down during a mission to Misburg.**

250680
V2

30

*Top:* **Nice shot of B-24J-150-CO 44-40241 of the 854th BS, named *The Hard Way*. This aircraft survived hostilities.**

*Bottom:* **Another Liberator that survived to return to the USA after the war was B-24J-145-CO 44-40114 *Paddy's Wagon*, from the 855th BS.**

*Top:* **Probably taken at Pueblo, Colorado, brand new B-24J-150-CO 44-40230 of the 491st BG became *Tung Hoi* of the 852nd BS and was scrapped at North Pickenham in January 1945 after the nose wheel collapsed on take-off.**

*Bottom:* **B-24J-5-FO 42-51493, a pathfinder lead ship with radome lowered and releasing a smoke marker and napalm bombs. This aircraft flew with the 854th BS.**

## 492nd BOMBARDMENT GROUP (H)

The 492nd Bomb Group came to England in April 1944 and was allocated the air base at North Pickenham, Norfolk. The first combat mission was flown on the 11th May 1944 to Mulhouse. After sustaining exceptionally heavy losses the Group was disbanded, becoming a special operations unit – *The Carpetbaggers* – at Harrington, Northamptonshire, the 801st Bombardment Group (Provisional) being renumbered. In its North Pickenham incarnation the Group is generally referred to as the 492nd BG (First Organisation).

Its final mission was on 7th August 1944. In the four months of its combat bombing career the group completed 84 missions dropping 3,757 tons of bombs and losing 57 of its Liberators. The 492nd's gunners claimed 21 enemy aircraft destroyed and three damaged.

**Group Markings**

White disc with insignia blue 'U' on upper surface of starboard wing on olive drab aircraft and a black disc with white 'U' on silver machines. Initially black discs were painted on the vertical tails with the intention of incorporating the white capital 'U', but when the order was received to change all tail markings in the 2nd Air Division, a black diagonal band was painted across the tail surface. For a short time some 'Libs' were operating with the band partially across the disc until the ground crews found time to erase the original markings.

Squadron code letters on the fuselage were grey on olive drab and black on silver, as follows:

856th Squadron '5Z -'
857th Squadron '9H -'
858th Squadron '9A -'
859th Squadron 'X4 -'

'Bars' (minus signs) and '+' signs were applied to the aircraft call-letters as follows:

856th Squadron no sign
857th Squadron 'bar' above
858th Squadron 'bar' below
859th Squadron '+' after

*Opposite page:*

*Top and centre:* **Two 492nd BG aircraft that suffered flak damage during the 11th July 1944 mission to Munich and sought sanctuary at Dübendorf, Switzerland: 856th BS B-24H-25-FO 42-95196, flown by Lt Paul Plantinski; and *Tequila Daisy*, a B-24J-150-CO 44-40168 of the 857th BS, piloted by Lt John C Tracey.**

*Bottom:* **Taken during the 492nd BG's mission to Saarbrücken on 16th July 1944 *Umbriago*, 44-40068, a B-24J-145-CO assigned to the 859th BS. It moved on to the 467th BG at Rackheath with several other of the Group's aircraft, when the 492nd was taken off bombing operations. The peculiar tail markings on *Umbriago* are explained by the fact that several 492nd BG aircraft were partially painted with the old style 'letter-in-circle' marking when in the spring of 1944 the new style black diagonal stripe group marking came into use. This was applied without the black circle being removed and with the serial number left on the outside of the fin.**

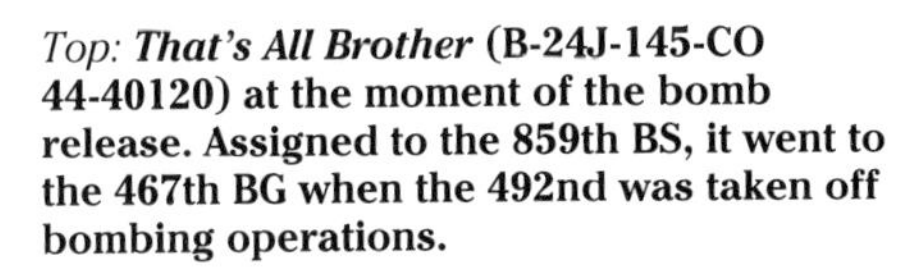

*Top:* ***That's All Brother*** **(B-24J-145-CO 44-40120) at the moment of the bomb release. Assigned to the 859th BS, it went to the 467th BG when the 492nd was taken off bombing operations.**

*Centre:* **Bombs cascade from *Urgin' Virgin*, B-24J-1-FO 42-50754, of the 491st BG's 853rd BS on to the Vomag tank works, Plauen, Germany on 5th April 1945. This is one of the few photographs showing 491st BG aircraft with 14th CBW tail markings.**

*Below:* **B-24J-155-CO 44-40317 *Ruthless Ruthie*, from the 854th BS, 491st BG. *Ruthie* blew a tyre on take-off for the mission of 16th April 1945 to the Landshut marshalling yards. The pilot was Lt Fuller.**

*Above:* **B-24J-1-DT 42-51258 of the 856th BS leaving the target. She was transferred to the 44th BG.**

*Centre left and below left:* **Two views of B-24J-55-CF 44-10496 of the 859th BS, damaged on the mission to Oberpfaffenhoffen on 21st July 1944, but which managed to limp into Dübendorf, Switzerland.**

*Opposite page:*

*Top:* **Early in 1944 *Lemon Drop* B-24D-1-CO 41-23699 was taken off operations and with armament removed and painted with yellow and black stripes became the 44th BG's assembly ship.**

*Centre:* **One of the most garish of the 2nd Air Division's assembly ships was the 392nd BG's B-24D-1-CO 41-23689 which originally flew as *Minerva* with the 44th BG. Towards the end of its long career, in April 1945, it carried no less than 52 men, plus their kit, in an experimental ten hour flight to find if it was feasible to airlift ground personnel home to the US after VE Day; an idea which was not taken up.**

*Bottom:* ***Tubarao* B-24J-145-CO 44-40101, formerly with the 854th BS, became the 491st BG's third and last assembly ship during January 1945 and remained so until VE Day.**

A
N

X

TUBARAO

**44th BOMBARDMENT GROUP:**

**Close up of the nose of B-24D-1-CO 41-23699 *Lemon Drop*, the 44th's assemble ship, showing the *Flying Eightball* logo. And, above, *Lemon Drop* nose-art when it served with the 68th BS.**

**B-24D-160-CO 42-72858 *Pistol Packin' Mama* of the 68th BS, force-landed Bulltofta, Sweden on 9th April 1944.**

**B-24D-25-CO 41-24232 *Calaban* of the 67th BS. It was lost on the Emden mission of 11th December 1943.**

*Opposite page:*

**B-24H-20-FO 42-95016 *Down 'De Hatch* of the 506th BS.**

**B-24D-5-CO 41-23813 *Victory Ship* of the 68th BS.**

**Lt 'Pete' Henry's aircraft, B-24J-155-CO 44-40279 *Henry* of the 66th BS. It survived the war.**

**B-24D-155-CO 42-72813 *Queen Marlene* of the 66th BS.**

**B-24H-1-FO 42-7476 *Nice 'N Naughty* of the 66th BS.**

**B-24H-1-FO 42-7535 *Peep Sight* of the 506th BS.**

DOWN 'DE HATCH

QUEEN
FIRE EXTINGUISHER
MARLENE

13
Victory Ship

NICE 'N
NAUGHTY.
FIRE EXTINGUISHER

HENRY

PEEP SIGHT

**392nd BOMBARDMENT GROUP**

**On 29th April 1944 the 392nd BG went to Berlin and lost eight aircraft. One of these was *Double Trouble*, a B-24J-70-CO (42-100100) of the 578th BS flown by 2/Lt G E Rogers.**

**B-24H-20-FO 42-94906 *Dragon Lady* of the 477th BS.**

**B-24J-1-FO 42-50697 *We'll Get By* of the 577th BS.**

**B-24H-1-FO 42-7466 *Fords' Folly*, assigned to the 578th BS. Compare the modification state of the nose to that on page 65.**

**B-24H-1-FO 42-7492 *Hell Wagon* of the 576th BS.**

**B-24H-25-FO 42-95037 *Sally* of the 579th BS.**

**392nd BOMBARDMENT GROUP:**

**B-24J-80-CO 42-100187 *Pallas Athene – The GI Jane*, 578th BS.**

**B-24H-1-FO 42-7546 *'Rob' Alfred II* of the 577th BS.**

**B-24H-15-FO 42-52770 *The Ruptured Duck* of 576th BS.**

**B-24H-25-FO 42-95164 *Lady Eve* of the 577th BS.**

***Birdie Schmidt*, B-24H-25-CF 42-50387, was named after the American Red Cross Aero Club hostess at Wendling.**

**B-24J-90-CO 42-100308 *Our Gal* of the 578th BS.**

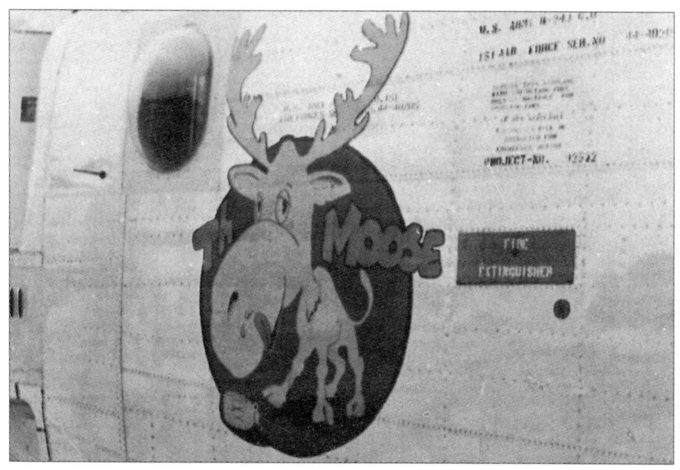


**491st BOMBARDMENT GROUP:**

**B-24J-150-CO 44-40226 *Mah Aikin Back* of the 854th BS. It force-landed in France on a mission to Hannover on 11th September 1944.**

**B-24J-155-CO 44-40271 *House of Rumor* of the 854th BS. The navigator's window mod has 'intruded' on the nose art.**

**B-24J-145-CO 44-40123 *She Devil* of the 852nd BS.**

**B-24J-145-CO 44-40084 *Little Joe* of the 854th BS.**

**B-24J-155-CO 44-40249 *Back to the Sack* of the 854th BS.**

**B-24J-150-CO 44-40205 *The Moose* of the 853rd BS.**

**492nd BOMBARDMENT GROUP:**

**B-24J-150-CO 44-40157 *Lucky Lass* assigned to the 857th BS, 492nd BG certainly lived up to her name for, on the Group's fifth mission, to Brunswick on 19th May 1944, *Lucky Lass* survived a mid-air collision with a German fighter, which lost a wing and crashed.**

**B-24J-145-CO 44-40125 *Herk's Jerks* flew with both the 858th and 857th Squadrons before being transferred to 389th BG.**

**B-24J-1-FO 42-50555 *Baby Shoes* flew eight missions with the 856th BS before transfer to the 458th BG at Horsham St Faith.**

***Bottle Baby*, B-24J-150-CO 44-40169 of the 858th BS which was shot down by fighters during the 492nd BG's ill-fated mission to Pölitz on 20th June 1944 when the group lost 14 aircraft.**

**B-24J-145-CO 44-40137 *What's Next Doc?* of the 857th BS.**

**B-24J-145-CO 44-40103 *Say When* of the 858th was badly damaged on the Pölitz mission and managed to make it to Bulltofta, Sweden.**

Chapter Four

# 20th Combat Bomb Wing

**93rd BOMBARDMENT GROUP (H)**
***Ted's Travelling Circus***

The 93rd Bomb Group – known as *Ted's Travelling Circus* – were initially housed at Alconbury, Huntingdonshire, arriving in the county in September 1942. The group flew its first combat mission from there on 9th October to the Fives-Lille steel works in Belgium. The Group then moved to Hardwick, Norfolk, where it remained throughout its service in the UK apart from three detachments made to North Africa in 1942-43.

The 93rd took part in the famous low-level mission to Ploesti for which it received a Distinguished Unit Citation and two of its pilots – Commanding Officer Lt Col Addison E Baker and Major John L Jerstad – were posthumously awarded the Congressional Medal of Honor.

The 93rd Bomb Group flew a total of 396 combat missions, a record for any 8th Air Force Heavy Bomber Group. These include the 41 missions undertaken during its three detachments to North Africa. A grand total of 19,004 tons of bombs were delivered by the Group. The 93rd BG lost 140 of its Liberators and its gunners claimed 93 enemy aircraft destroyed, 41 probables, 44 damaged. Its last mission was flown 25th April 1945.

## Group Markings

During the Group's first detachment to North Africa, RAF-style fin flashes were painted on both sides of their vertical tail surfaces and many aircraft retained these until the white disc markings were applied. No group markings were carried until August/September 1943 when a white disc was painted on the vertical tail surfaces and starboard upper wingtip with an insignia blue capital 'B' within the disc. In May 1944 the tails were painted a deep yellow with a black vertical stripe. Squadron code letters were grey on olive drab aircraft and black on silver machines. A 'bar' above or below the call-letter was used to denote aircraft with the same call-letter within the Group – this stopped when the tail colours and stripes were introduced.

| | |
|---|---|
| 328th Squadron | 'GO-' |
| 329th Squadron | 'RE-' |
| 330th Squadron | 'AG-' |
| 409th Squadron | 'YM-' |

Many 330th Squadron's aircraft carried a distinctive whale mouth on their noses and later in the war the 409th Squadron carried deep yellow spinners and cowl rings.

Pathfinder aircraft in the 329th Squadron had their noses painted red from late summer 1944. Beyond January 1945, 328th PFF ships had their noses painted in deep yellow with black chequerboards. It is likely that the other two squadrons also had chequerboard noses for their PPF aircraft, but at the time of going to press, this could not be confirmed.

*Photograph(s) opposite and on this page:*

**Ordnance men of the 93rd Bomb Group preparing 1,000lb bombs prior to loading B-24Ds *Eager Beaver* and *Katy Bug* (B-24D-1-CO 41-23745) at the 93rd's first English base at Alconbury. These photos show well the early nose armament of three 0.50 calibre machine guns. In combat the lower gun proved rather ineffective with a restricted field of fire as it could be depressed but not elevated. The problem was partially solved by moving the weapon further up the transparency and in some cases adding a second gun.**

123744
GERONIMO

*Opposite page:*

*Top:* ***Geronimo***, **B-24D-1-CO 41-23744, bogged down after a nose-wheel collapse at Tafaroui, Algeria, on the 14th December, 1942 during the 93rd's first detachment to North Africa. North American B-25 Mitchells in the background.**

*Bottom:* **A formation of 93rd Bomb Group B-24Ds in the Mediterranean sunshine during their detachment to North Africa for Operation 'Torch'. Nearest is** ***Bomerang*****. The irregular green blotching along the leading and trailing edges of the wings and tail assembly was applied to most 8th AF B-24s during the autumn of 1942.**

*This page:*

*Right:* **B-24D-1-CO 41-23672** ***Double Trouble*** **squats on her hardstand. She flew with the 328th BS until lost on a mission to Sousse, Tunisia, on 19th January 1943.**

*Below:* **Undergoing maintenance on its hardstand at Hardwick in April 1943, the 93rd's B-24D-1-CO 41-23729** ***Shoot Luke*****. This aircraft, which flew with the 328th BS carries RAF-type fin flashes.**

*Left and centre left:* **Two views of the 93rd BG practising low level flying over England during preparations for the Ploesti mission of 1st August, 1943. The upper photograph shows *Jerks Natural* (B-24D-1-CO 41-23711) leading B-24D-15-CO 41-23990, *Heinie Hunter*, nearest the camera.**

**B-24D-20-CF 42-63974 of the 93rd BG which crash-landed at Watton airfield, Norfolk in November 1943. It carries on the nose the panda bear insignia of the 409th BS.**

*Opposite page:*

*Top:* **The 93rd BG's *Hellsadroppin II* landing at Hardwick in the summer of 1943. This aircraft, B-24D-5-CO 41-23809, carried the national insignia outlined in red, a style used for only a brief period before it was changed to the familiar blue. *Hellsadroppin II* later became the 448th BG's assembly ship and was renamed *You Cawn't Miss It*.**

*Centre:* **Nearly new B-24H-1-FO 42-7519 of the 93rd BG tied down in the snow at Dübendorf, Switzerland. It force-landed there on 7th January, 1944 during a mission to Ludwigshafen. Nose art has been applied in white outline only, never to be completed.**

*Bottom:* **The 93rd BG's famous *Bomerang*, B-24D-1-CO 41-23722 of the 328th BS, was the first 8th Air Force Liberator to complete 50 missions. It returned to the US after three more missions for a War Bond tour. In the photograph the censor has obscured the anti-flash muzzles on the machine guns which presumably indicates that the aircraft was used, at some time, for night operations.**

B
N

B
27519
D

B
2100294
B

B
AG
H
Big Moise

*Opposite page:*

*Top:* **A pair of 93rd BG B-24J-90-COs *en route* to Germany. The lower Liberator, 42-100294, then on its fifth mission, later was named *Victory Belle*.**

*Bottom:* **On 16th March 1944 the 8th Air Force despatched 700 heavy bombers to attack aircraft factories in southern Germany. They met severe fighter opposition and seven damaged B-17s and B-24s crashed or force-landed in Switzerland. One of these was the 93rd BG's *Big Noise*, B-24D-120-CO 42-40969 of the 330th BS, in the snow at Dübendorf.**

*This page:*

*Right:* **B-24D-120-CO 42-40990 *On the Ball* of the 93rd, climbing to altitude. She was lost over France on 7th January 1944.**

*Below:* **Two B-24Hs tucking it in tight. The nearest aircraft, B-24H-1-DT 41-28626 *'218' Thunderbird* was lost on 5th February 1944 when it crashed in Paris. B-24H-1-FO 42-7499 *De Boid,* in the background, survived the war.**

B
2110081
A
GO

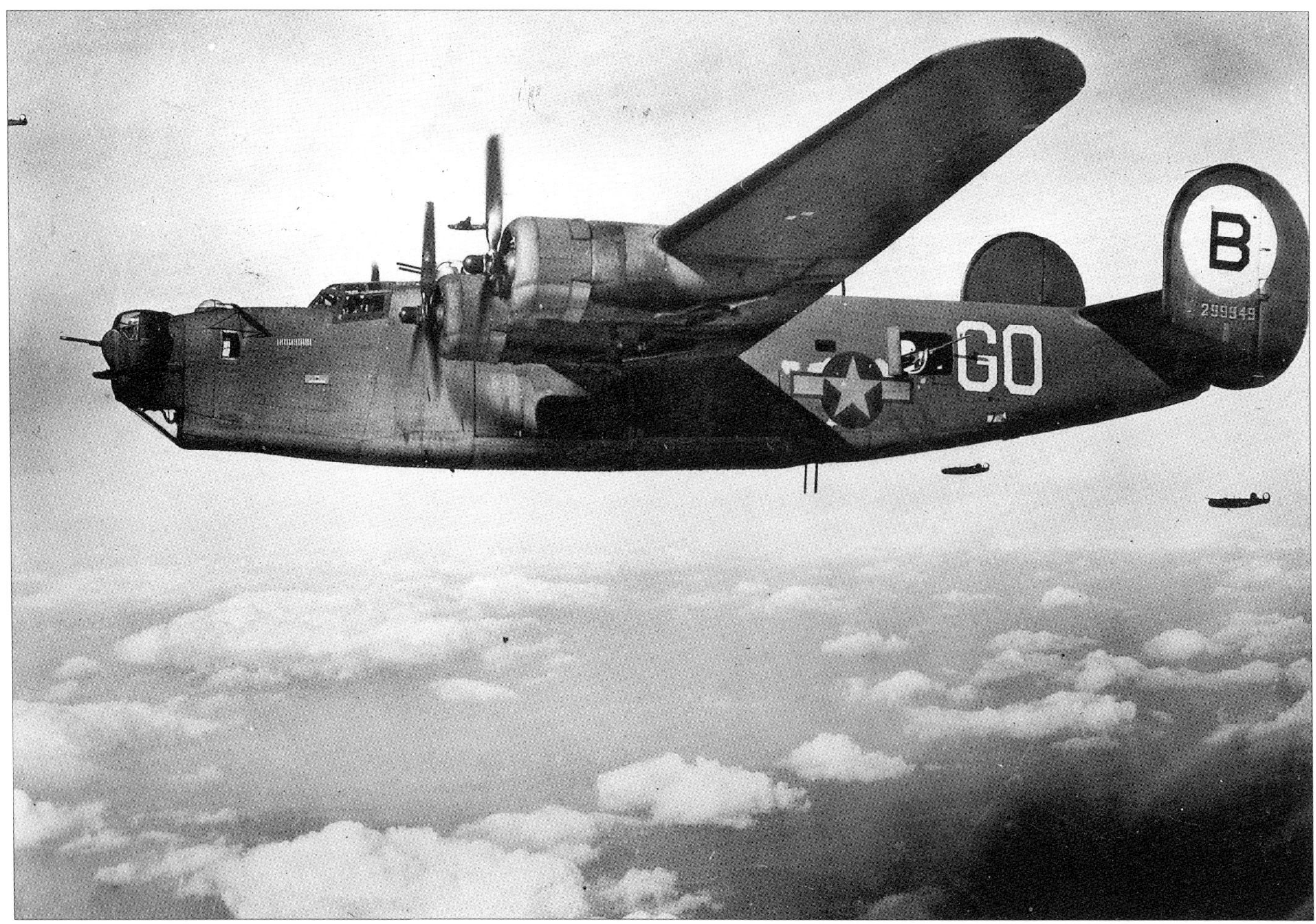
B
299949
GO

*Top:* **The classic lines of the B-24's high-aspect ratio Davis wing displayed by a 93rd BG Liberator over an enemy target.**

*Centre right:* **B-24J-130-CO 42-110072 of the 330th BS, 93rd BG, crash-landed at Hardwick after the starboard undercarriage leg collapsed. Note the smoke-marker canister on the external rack under the starboard wing.**

*Bottom:* **B-24J-5-FO 42-50829 of the 93rd BG. It is decorated with a 'whale-mouth' nose which became a form of marking carried by most aircraft of the 330th BS.**

*Opposite page:*

*Top:* **B-24J-130-CO 42-110081 *Able Mabel* cruises at altitude. *Mabel* was lost over Belgium on 19th June 1944. She displays her newly applied codes for the 328th Bomb Squadron on her fuselage.**

*Bottom:* **B-24J-55-CO 42-99949 *Naughty Nan* of the 328th BS, 93rd BG, cruises above cloud, waist guns deployed.**

*Top:* **Several 2nd Air Division Liberators were decorated with dragon noses. B-24J-5-DT 42-51376 of the 93rd BG's 329th BS survived the war.**

*Centre left:* **A fine shot of a B-24H from the 328th BS banking over the Norfolk countryside near the 93rd BG's base at Hardwick.**

*Bottom:* **Deep yellow and black chequer nose on Tulsa-built B-24J *Unexpected VI* taxying at Hardwick, indicates that it was fitted with blind bombing equipment and flew with the 93rd's 328th Squadron. The 329th pathfinders carried red noses.**

*Opposite page:*

*Top:* **B-24J-15-FO 42-51968 from the 93rd's 329th BS, a PFF aircraft with radome extended and bomb doors open, nears the target, in heavy flak .**

*Bottom:* **A formation of B-24s of the 93rd BG's 329th BS; nearest is B-24J-145-CO 44-40113 *Gambling Lady*. Traces of the old 857th BS code '9H' can be seen beneath the new code 'RE'.**

P

RE
K

*Left:* **Two B-24s of the 409th BS, 93rd BG, in flak *en route* to Augsburg, 1st March 1945: B-24J-5-DT 42-51305 with B-24H-25-FO 42-95204 *Down and Go* in the background. This shows well two typical features of a fully-laden Liberator in flight, the 'nose-up' attitude and the pronounced upward curvature of the Davis wing.**

*Bottom:* **Two 93rd BG aircraft over the southern Alps during the last few weeks of the war in Europe. Nearest camera is B-24M-5-FO 44-50579 of the 328th BS, in company with a B-24L of the 329th BS.**

*Opposite page:*

*Top:* **Smoke markers go down over Zossen, Germany, past B-24M-5-FO 44-50537 of the 93rd BG's 328th BS, during the raid of 15th March, 1945 on the German High Command HQ.**

*Bottom:* **For a period lasting from 30th August until 9th September 1944, 8th Air Force Liberators were used to ferry food and medical supplies to France. Seen at Orléans are 330th BS B-24H-25-FO 42-95046 with *Big Noise II* behind.**

GO
F

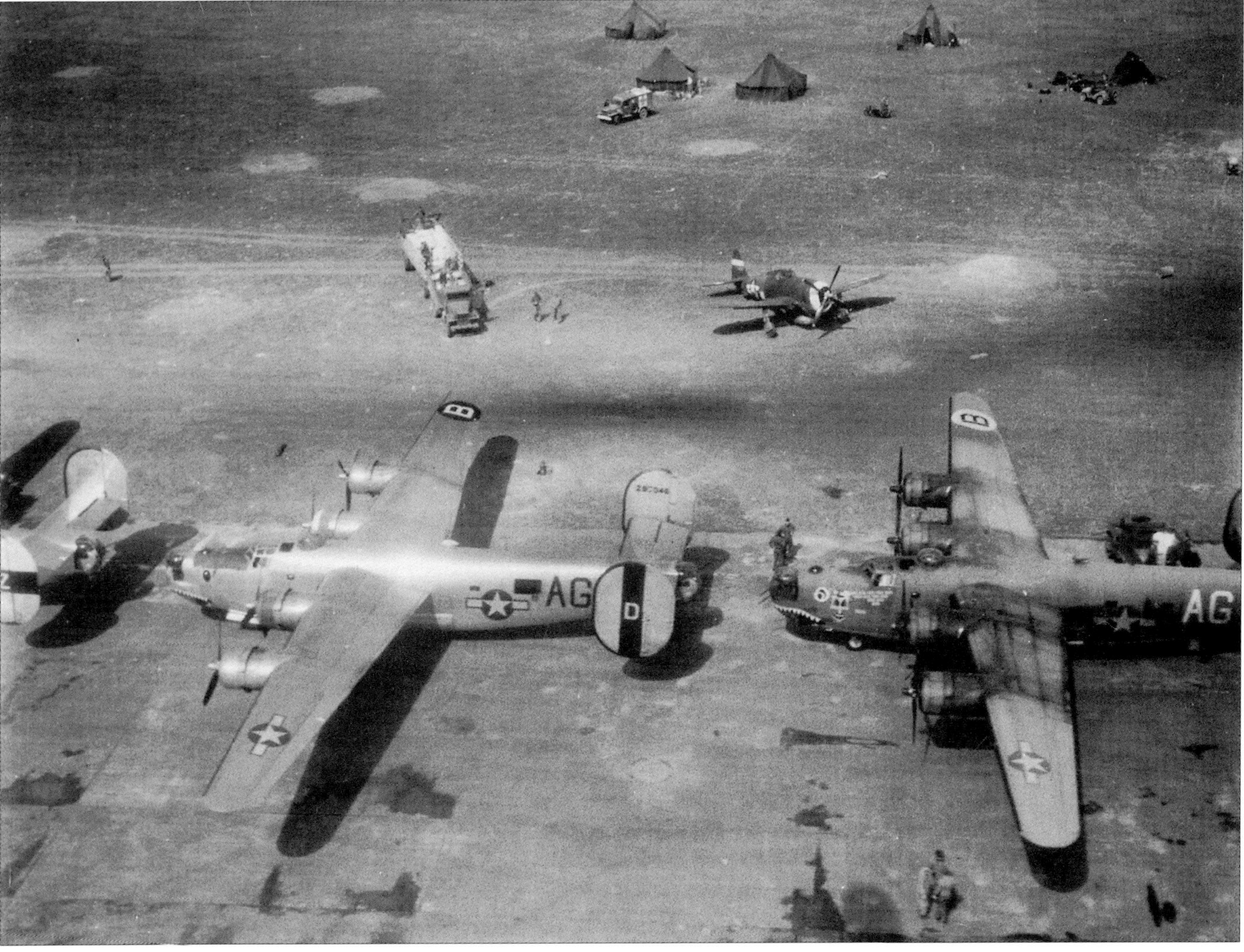
AG
D
AG

*Above:* **Nice shot of two 409th BS 'Libs' high over the North Sea. 'YM-N' is B-24J-401-CF 42-50485 *O-Bit-U-Airy-Mary* whilst 'YM-Q' is B-24H-25-CF 42-50372. Both of these B-24s survived the war.**

*Below:* **Tight formation of 93rd BG B-24Hs on a low level training mission over southern England.**

**446th BOMBARDMENT GROUP (H)**
***Bungay Buckeroos***

The 446th BG were assigned to the 8th Air Force in November 1943. They flew their first mission to Bremen, Germany on 16th December 1943. The group operated from Bungay, Suffolk, and flew a total of 273 combat missions and dropped a total of 16,819 tons of bombs. The *Buckeroos* lost a total of 86 Liberators and claimed 34 enemy aircraft destroyed, eleven probables and eight damaged.

**Group Markings**
An insignia blue capital 'H' superimposed on a white disc on the upper starboard wingtip and outer vertical tail surfaces, was worn until May 1944 when the tails were painted deep yellow with a black horizontal stripe. Late in the war H2S lead ships had a black ring superimposed over existing tail markings.

The squadron codes were grey on olive drab and black on silver:
704th Squadron 'FL -'
705th Squadron 'HN -'
706th Squadron 'RT -'
707th Squadron 'JU -
'Bars' (minus signs) were used with call-letters until the tail striping and colours were employed:
704th Squadron no sign
705th Squadron 'bar' below
706th Squadron 'bar' above
707th Squadron 'bar' above and below
From about June 1944 coloured cowl bands were carried on the engines:
red for the 704th
yellow for the 705th
white for the 706th
blue for the 707th.

*Top:* **A pair of B-24H-1-FOs. Closest is 42-7609 *Lazy Lou* of the 446th BG with 42-7655 of the 93rd BG.**

*Centre right:* **Led by a pathfinder aircraft of the 482nd BG, with H2S radome replacing the ball turret, a formation of 446th BG B-24Hs en route to Europe early in 1944. Aircraft include B-24H-1-CF 41-29141 *Kill Joy*** *(bottom centre)*, ***Werewolf*** *(top left)* **with *Stardust* just below.**

*Right:* ***Merle Lee*, B-24H-1-FO 42-7584 of the 446th Bomb Group, somewhat worse for wear after crash-landing at Hawkinge, Kent, in January 1944.**

*Above:* **Friedrichshafen was the target for the 8th Air Force on18th March 1944 and nearby Switzerland became the refuge for no less than 16 B-17s and B-24s damaged by flak or fighters. Two 20th CBW Liberators force-landed at Dübendorf including 446th BG B-24H-1-FO 42-7625. Note the feathered prop on No.4 engine on '625 and the crashed B-17 in the background.**

*Below:* **A mixed formation of B-24Hs and 'Js of the 446th BG. Nearest the camera is B-24J-95-CO 42-100360 *Luck and Stuff* showing the ventral ball turret in the retracted position. In the late summer of 1944 many 2nd AD B-24s had these turrets removed to save weight and thereby give better performance.**

*Opposite page:*

*Top:* **Experimental release of a fragmentation cluster from B-24J-95-CO 42-100347 of the 707th BS 446th BG on 1st May 1944. *Lil' Max* was lost over Holland on 26th September 1944.**

*Bottom:* ***Dry Run*, a B-24H-1-CF (41-29137) of the 446th BG.**

H
JU

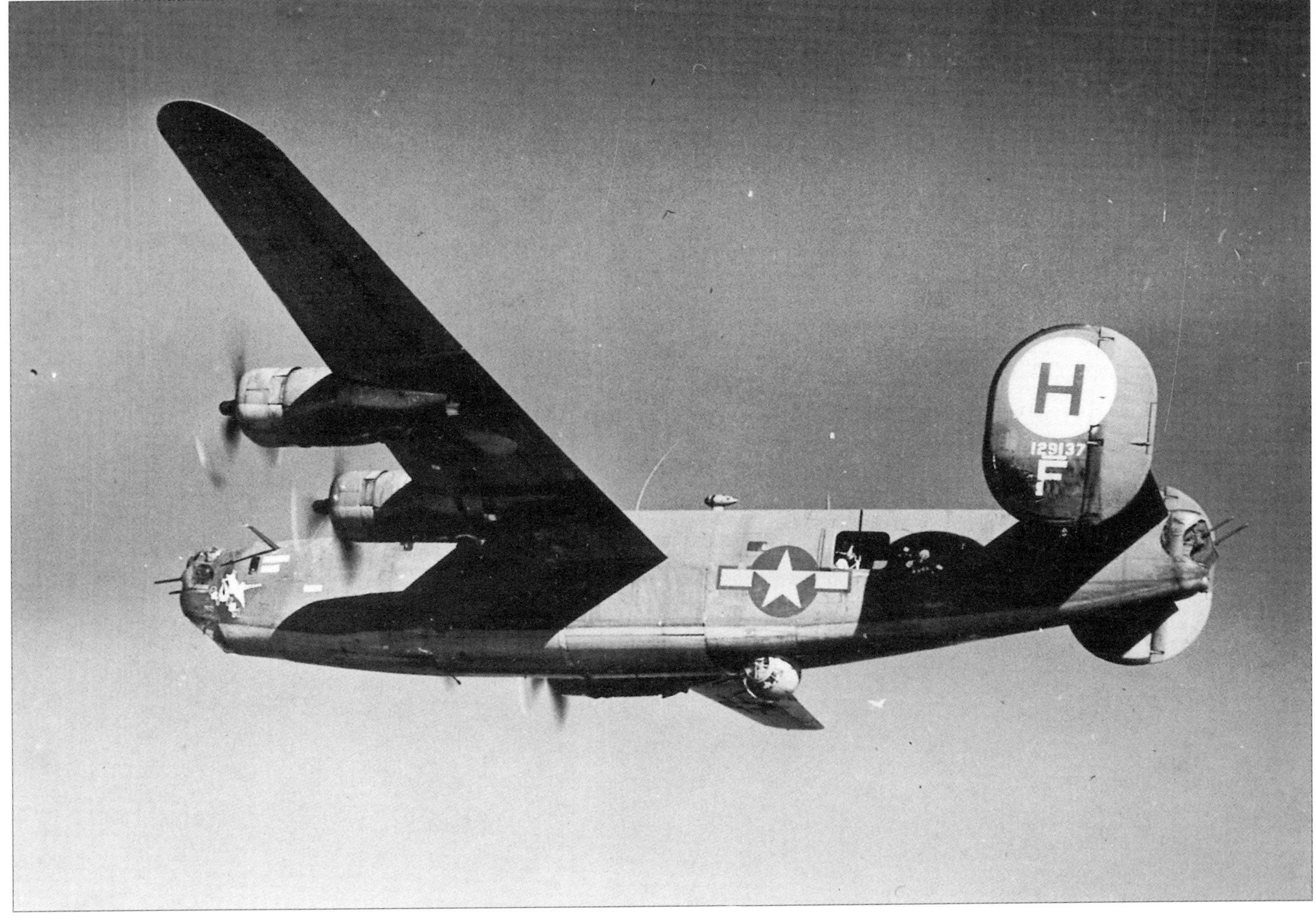
H
129137
F

*Opposite page:*

*Top:* **The 446th BG forming over the North Sea with *Old-Faithful,* B-24H-1-FO 42-7505 in the foreground, *Lazy Lou* above and *The Spirit of 77* below.**

*Bottom:* **On the day before D-Day, 5th June 1944, the 20th CBW were assigned targets in Northern France. The 446th BG attacked Calais and 42-7609 *Lazy Lou* of the 706th BS in company with three 705th BS aircraft are shown just after bomb release. The newly added coloured cowl bands, yellow for 705th BS, white for 706th BS, show up clearly.**

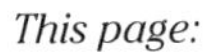

*This page:*

*Top:* ***Lil Snooks*, B-24H-20-FO 42-94936, from the 707th BS, 446th BG.**

*Centre:* **One of the most famous Liberators in the 2nd Air Division was the 446th BG's *Ronnie*. A B-24H-1-CF, 41-29144 was assigned to the 704th BS and was named after one of the original crew, S/Sgt Ronald Gannon, who contracted a fatal illness when the group were in training in the US. *Ronnie* survived the war completing 119 missions, to join that select band of 2nd AD centenarians.**

*Right:* **Showing signs of its long service with the 706th BS of 446th BG is *Homebreaker*, B-24H-15-FO 42-52612, on its 100th mission, to Rechlin airfield, on 10th April 1945.**

H
N
B
YM

H

*Opposite page:*

Top: **Line-up of B-24s unloading flour at Orléans, 3rd September 1944. In the middle is *Naughty Nan*, B-24H-15-FO 42-52594 of the 446th BG. This is a wholly different *Nan* from that on page 98.**

*Bottom:* **B-24H-1-FO 42-7576 *Stardust* of the 705th BS.**

*This page:*

*Above:* ***The Spirit of 77*, B-24H-1-FO 42-7607 of the 446th BG's 705th Squadron with bar below the call-letter and ball turret deployed.**

*Below:* **B-24J-5-FO 42-50814 of the 706th BS leads a 446th Bomb Group formation over the patchwork fields of East Anglia.**

RED
ASS

RT
H

251203
RT
R

*Opposite page:*

*Top:* ***Red Ass*****, B-24H-25-FO 42-95203, of the 704th BS, 446th BG *****en route***** to Hanau, Germany, on 10th November 1944.**

*Centre:* **B-24J-155-CO 44-40268 from the 706th BS 446th BG on the Bottrop mission of 11th November 1944. This aircraft was later given the name *****Kentucky Belle*****.**

*Bottom:* **B-24H-30-DT 42-51203 was assigned to the 706th BS of the 446th BG.**

*This page:*

*Top and centre right:* ***Patriotic Patty*****, B-24J-1-FO 42-50734, from the 707th BS, 446th BG. In the airborne view, *****Patty***** is shown during a support mission for the Rhine crossing on 24th March 1945. Note that the guns have been removed from the nose turret and waist windows.**

*Centre left:* ***Bar Fly***** of the 707th BS with other 446th BG aircraft on the Nürnberg mission of 21st February 1945.**

*Bottom right:* **Two B-24s of the 446th BG's 707th BS en route to Magdeburg on the 6th February 1945. The lower aircraft is *****Going My Way*****, B-24J-60-CF 44-10528, normally flown by Lt Carl Cjelhaug.**

*Above:* **The last moments before bomb release for B-24J-5-FO 42-50773 *Queenie* from the 446th BG's 707th BS, over the rail yards at Aschaffenburg, Germany on 25th February 1945.**

*Below:* **Bombs fall away from B-24M-5-FO 44-50517 of the 707th BS, 446th BG, over Passau on 18th April 1945.**

*Above:* **The 446th BG flew to Salzburg on its final mission on 25th April 1945 and on that mission was B-24J-5-FO 42-50882 *Wolf Patrol*, of the 705th BS, shown just after bomb release.**

*Right:* **B-24-25-H-FO 42-95059 *Shady Sadie* raises a puff of white smoke from her tyres as she touches down at Flixton.**

*Below:* **Three 706th Bomb Squadron 'Libs' head for their objective with a PFF 'Mickey Ship' in the lead. The nearest aircraft is B-24H-30-DT 42-51203.**

## 448th BOMBARDMENT GROUP (H)

This Group came to England in November 1943 and moved into its base at Seething, Norfolk, from where it flew its first combat mission to Osnabrück, Germany on 22nd December 1943. The 448th went on to complete 262 missions and dropped 15,272 tons of ordnance. It lost 135 Liberators and claimed 44 enemy aircraft destroyed, 19 probables and 30 damaged.

### Group Markings

The 448th carried the usual white disc on the upper starboard wingtip and on the tail surfaces with a capital 'I' within this disc in insignia blue. The Group did not conform to normal practise and adopted a squadron symbol to surround their aircraft's call-letter on the lower half of the fin painted in deep yellow to conform with the call-letter:

| | |
|---|---|
| 712th Squadron | triangle |
| 713th Squadron | circle |
| 714th Squadron | square |
| 715th Squadron | diamond |

In May 1944 the outer surfaces of the tail were painted deep yellow with a black diagonal band with the call-letter and symbol superimposed on this band. The letter and symbol was also carried on the inner sides of the fin. Later a large call-letter only was used on the inner fin.

Squadron letters were grey on olive drab and black on silver. Later in the war many 448th machines flew without squadron code letters. Squadron codes were:

| | |
|---|---|
| 712th Squadron | 'CT -' |
| 713th Squadron | 'IG -' |
| 714th Squadron | 'EI -' |
| 715th Squadron | 'IO -' |

*Left:* ***Hello Natural II*, B-24H-15-FO 42-52606, of the 712th BS, 448th BG, sits on the hardstand at Seething.**

*Centre left:* ***Fatstuff II* of the 448th BG taxies back to its hardstand at Seething after the 22nd March 1944 mission to Berlin. This aircraft, B-24H-1-FO 42-7591 'J' of the 712th BS, force-landed at Altenrhein, Switzerland after a raid on Munich on 12th July 1944.**

*Below:* **Switzerland became the refuge for no less than 16 B-17s and B-24s damaged by flak or fighters following a raid on Friedrichshafen on 18th March 1944. Two 20th CBW Liberators force-landed at Dübendorf including B-24J-85-CO 42-100284 of the 714th BS 448th BG. Note evidence of a scrubbed out nose-art.**

*Top:* **B-24J-135-CO 42-110098 *The Flying Sac* of the 448th BG which force-landed at Dübendorf, Switzerland on April 24th 1944. It carries the squadron marking unique to the 448th BG of the geometric figure enclosing the aircraft's individual call-letter, in this case a diamond denoting the 715th BS.**

*Right, second down:* **An interesting photo of *Poop Deck Pappy* an early Ford-built B-24H of the 448th BG's 714th BS showing the Motor Products A-6 hydraulic turret in the nose instead of the standard electrically-driven Emerson type. Previously illustrated on page 62, the aircraft has been much modified, showing to great effect how 'field' modifications were brought in.**

*Right, third down:* ***Dead End Kids*, B-24H-20-FO 42-94992, of the 713th BS, 448th BG undergoing repairs at 3rd Strategic Air Depot, Griston, Norfolk, May 1945.**

*Bottom, left and right:* **With feathered propellers on No.1 and No.3 engines the 448th BG's 712th BS *Little Sheppard*, B-24H-10-DT 41-28711, force-landed at Dübendorf, Switzerland on 21st July 1944.**

*Above:* **Garishly decorated B-24H-20-FO 42-94953 *Rugged But Right* from the 715th Bomb Squadron, 448th Bomb Group, coming in to land at Seething.**

*Centre left:* **A later view of *Rugged But Right*, with the 'face' painted yellow.**

*Bottom left:* **713th BS B-24H-1-DT 41-28583 *Rum Runner,* down at Dübendorf in Switzerland on 25th April 1944.**

*Opposite page:*

*Top:* **The 448th BG sets out on one of its early missions. Nearest is *Lady From Bristol*, B-24H-5-FO 42-52100, from the 714th BS. She was lost on 25th February 1944, south east of Amiens, France.**

*Bottom:* **Billowing clouds provide the backdrop to B-24H-20-CF 41-28958 *Little Jo* and other B-24s of the 713th BS, 448th BG on their way to Germany.**

*Top left:* **Three 715th BS 'Libs' in formation on an early mission. Nearest is B-24H-5-FO 42-7764 *Bag of Bolts* with B-24J-50-CO 42-73512 off the starboard wing.**

*Below, centre left:* ***Shady Lady*, B-24J-1-FO 42-50759, of the 448th BG which crash-landed at RAF Lissett, Yorkshire, in November 1944. Squadron codes were removed from 448th BG aircraft during the autumn of 1944.**

*Below, centre right:* **Moment of bomb release from two B-24s of the 714th BS, 448th BG. Nearest aircraft is a B-24J-5-FO, 42-50809. The two bulges under the forward fuselage are covers for the radio countermeasures (RCM) antennas which were installed in many 2nd AD B-24s later in the war.**

*Bottom:* **B-24J-5-FO 42-51075 *Linda Mae* over Reedham Church. She survived the war.**

*Top:* **B-24J-1-FO 42-95527 *4-F* – its name, not a code – of the 712th BS.**

*Centre left and right:* **Republic P-47C-5-RE 41-6380 used by the 448th as a formation monitor. It is seen in two guises, both carrying the 'whale mouth', but left with D-Day strips and a broad white band across the fin and rudder, the latter minus the D-Day markings but including the 448th's yellow fin and rudder plus black diagonal stripe.**

*Bottom:* **B-24H-25-FO 42-95083 *My Buddie* rests on its hardstand. It went on to survive the hostilities.**

## 489th BOMBARDMENT GROUP (H)

The 489th crossed the Atlantic in April 1944 and stayed in England for only eight months, returning to the USA in November to train on the new Boeing B-29 Superfortresses.

It was originally part of the 95th Combat Wing but was re-assigned to the 20th Combat Wing in August 1944. Based at Halesworth, Suffolk, the 489th flew its first mission to Oldenburg, Germany on 30th May and went on to complete 106 missions, its last mission being flown on 10th November 1944. The group dropped a total of 6,951 tons of bombs, lost 41 B-24s and claimed one enemy aircraft destroyed.

The 489th's Deputy Commander, Lt Col Leon Vance Jr, was awarded the Congressional Medal of Honour for his heroism on 5th June 1944.

### Group Markings

White disc containing capital 'W' on upper starboard wingtip. Vertical tail surfaces painted green with white vertical stripe (95th Combat Wing markings) until August 1944 when tails were painted yellow.

'Bars' and '+' signs were used with call-letters until the tail striping and colours were employed.

| | |
|---|---|
| 844th Squadron | no sign |
| 845th Squadron | 'bar' before or below |
| 846th Squadron | '+' after |
| 847th Squadron | 'bar' above or after |

Code letters on the fuselage were grey on the olive drab aircraft and black on the silver aircraft:

| | |
|---|---|
| 844th Squadron | '4R -' |
| 845th Squadron | 'T4 -' |
| 846th Squadron | '8R -' |
| 847th Squadron | 'S4 -' |

*Below:* **Carrying the old green and white tail colours of the 95th Combat Wing, *The Sharon D*, B-24H-15-FO 42-94759, of the 845th BS, is seen over the blazing Misburg oil refinery on 12th September 1944. The 95th CBW had ceased to exist during the previous month and all the 489th BG's aircraft were eventually given the all-yellow tail colour denoting the new assignment to the 20th CBW.**

*Above:* **Vertical shot of the 489th BG's *Bomber's Moon*, B-24H-20-FO 42-94903, of the 844th BS, as it nears the target during the 3rd October 1944 mission to Speyerdorf airfield, Germany.**

*Right:* ***Lonesome Polecat*, B-24H-20-FO 42-94857, from the 846th BS, 489th BG, which crashed on Beccles marshes in early October 1944.**

*Below:* ***Special Delivery*, B-24H-20-FO 42-94896, and *Jo*, B-24H-15-FO 42-94783, both of the 489th's 845th BS, on the way to Münster on 25th October 1944.**

*Left:* **Two Liberators of the 844th BS, 489th BG en route to Münster on 25th October 1944. Nearest aircraft is B-24H-30-CF 42-50451 *Satan's Sister*, the last Fort Worth built 'H, flying above *The Sack*.**

*Below, centre left:* **With her new yellow tail gleaming in the sunlight *Rum Dum*, B-24H-20-CF 42-502-80, from the 845th Squadron in formation with friends.**

*Below, centre right:* **B-24H-25-DT 42-51120 *Ol' Buddy* of the 844th BS.**

*Bottom:* ***Rebel Gal*, B-24H-20-FO 42-94838, of the 845th Squadron taxies past a visiting 3rd Division 'Lib'.**

*Opposite page:*

**The 93rd BG assembly ship *Ball of Fire*, is veteran B-24D-1-CO 41-23667. Painted in gaudy red, white and pale blue stripes, this aircraft was used to assist formation build-ups in assembly areas. Her plumage underwent a gradual metamorphosis over the months, starting out as olive drab, white and yellow stripes, then red, white and yellow stripes, and finally narrow red and white stripes. In the centre photograph *Ball of Fire* is over Hempnall village, Norfolk.**

B
123667
H

B
123667
H

BALL OF FIRE
8

*Above, left and bottom left:* **The 446th BG's overall International Orange assembly ship *Fearless Freddie* (41-23737), formerly *Eager Beaver* of the 93rd BG.**

*Bottom right:* **The 489th BG forming up around their polka-dotted assembly ship *Lil Cookie*, a B-24H which formerly flew with the 44th BG. Nearest is *Fords' Folly*.**

*Opposite page:*

*Top:* **Resplendent in her yellow and black chequers, the 448th BG's first assembly ship, *You Cawn't Miss It,* was formerly the 93rd BG's *Hellsadropping II.***

*Centre and bottom:* **B-24H-15-CF 41-29489 in maroon and white stripes divided by black bands, replaced *You Cawn't Miss It* from January 1945, as the 448th's assembly ship.**

I

W

**93rd BOMBARDMENT GROUP:**

**The 93rd BG's *Wham Bam*, B-24D-1-CO 41-23738, flew with the 330th BS and later became the 453rd BG's assembly ship.**

***War Baby* (B-24D-30-CO 42-40128) force-landed at Orebro, Sweden, on 18th November 1943, after a raid on Kjeller airfield, Norway.**

***Victory Belle*, B-24J-90-CO 42-100294 of the 93rd BG. Note the 15 mission symbols and the navigator's scanning window of a type which became standard later in the war on Ford-built B-24Ls & 'Ms.**

***Iron Ass,* B-24D-95-CO 42-40769 went 'missing-in-action' on 1st December 1943.**

**B-24D-5-CO 41-23809 *Hellsadroppin II* of the 329th BS, later transferred to the 448th BG to become that Group's assembly ship *You Cawn't Miss It*.**

**B-24J-90-CO 42-100334 *Patches* of the 409th BS. She was lost on the 5th March 1945 mission to the synthetic oil plant at Ruhland.**

**93rd BOMBARDMENT GROUP:**

**B-24H-20-FO 42-94880 *Mischief* of the 330th BS. A former 34th BG aircraft, she survived hostilities.**

**B-24J-401-CF (42-50501) *Solid Comfort*, flew with the 330th BS and lasted out the war.**

**B-24J-100-CO 42-100413 *Satan's Sister II* of the 409th and 329th Squadrons. She was salvaged battle-damaged on the Continent on 27th December 1944.**

**B-24H-25-FO 42-95199, *The Latrine Rumor*, flew with both the 329th and 409th squadrons and survived.**

**B-24J-401-CF 42-50505, *The Gremlins Roost* from the 330th BS, was shot down over Holland on the Magdeburg mission on 6th February 1945.**

**B-24J-110-CO 42-109867 *Maulin' Mallard* of the 330th BS, survived the war with 104 missions credited.**

**446th BOMBARDMENT GROUP:**

**B-24H-15-FO 42-52594 *Naughty Nan* from the 705th BS.**

**B-24H-1-FO 42-7505 *Old-Faithful* of the 446th BG.**

**Practically every Bomb Group in the 8th Air Force had a *Piccadilly Commando* – named after those famous London 'ladies'. This one was B-24H-1-CF 41-29155, assigned to the 707th BS.**

**The 446th BG's *Star Dust*, B-24H-1-FO 42-7576, of the 705th BS. The armour plate below the cockpit windows was added as a field modification to most 8th Air Force B-24s.**

**B-24H-20-FO 42-94936 *Lil Snooks* from the 707th BS.**

**One of the better examples of 8th Air Force nose-art was that of *Classy Chassy,* a B-24H-25-FO (42-95198) of the 704th BS. This aircraft formerly flew with the 487th BG.**

**446th BOMBARDMENT GROUP:**

**B-24H-1-CF 41-29144 *Ronnie* of the 704th BS.**

**B-24H-1-CF 41-29125 *Tar Heel Baby* of the 707th Squadron.**

**B-24J-95-CO 42-100347 *Lil Max* from the 707th Squadron was lost over Holland on 26th September 1944.**

**B-24H-1-FO 42-7498 *Desperate Desmond* of the 706th BS was salvaged as 'war weary' on 29th May 1945.**

**B-24H-15-CF 41-29411 *Ridge Runner* from the 704th Squadron crashed and burned on 25th October 1944 on a local flight.**

**B-24J-105-CO 42-109830, *Daisy Mae Scraggs* of the 704th BS, was lost on 8th June 1944 in the English Channel.**

**446th BOMBARDMENT GROUP** *(left hand column)* :

**B-24H-25-FO 42-95180 *Satan's Little Sister,* 706th BS.**

**B-24H-25-FO 42-95203 *Red Ass* of the 704th BS.**

**B-24M-10-FO 44-50775 *Mighty Mouse* of the 704th BS.**

**448th BOMBARDMENT GROUP** *(right hand column)* :

***Hello Natural II*, B-24H-15-FO 42-52606, of the 712th BS, 448th BG. In addition to several flak patches, it features the field modification window in the navigator's position.**

**B-24J-50-CO 42-73477 *Feather Merchant* of the 714th BS. She was later assigned to the 492nd BG (2nd Organisation).**

***Back to the Sack* a B-24J-1-DT 42-51288 from the 714th BS.**

**B-24H-10-FO 42-52121 *Wolf Pack* of the 713th BS.**

*See page 173 for more nose-art from the 20th Combat Bomb Wing in 'Nose-Art Reprise'.*

Chapter Five

# 96th Combat Bomb Wing

**Something of an ugly beast on the ground, the Liberator in its natural element was a different matter as shown graphically by B-24H-15-CF 41-29408 from the 790th BS 467th BG. Standard wear and tear on the leading edges, whip aerials and the slipstream deflectors for the waist guns are also well apparent.**

## 458th BOMBARDMENT GROUP (H)

The 458th came over to England in early February 1944 and were allocated the former RAF airfield at Horsham St Faith (which is now Norwich Airport) on the outskirts of Norwich. The Group flew a diversionary mission on 24th February and its first combat mission to Frankfurt on the 2nd March.

The group completed 240 missions and dropped 13,204 tons of ordnance; 65 Liberators were lost and the Group claimed 28 enemy aircraft destroyed, three probables and 14 damaged. The last mission was flown on 25th April 1945.

During May 1944 the 753rd Squadron was selected to carry out the operational testing of the 'Azon' (azimuth only) bombing technique. A conventional bomb was fitted with a special tail section that responded to radio inputs from the 'mother ship' (see page 146 for the aerials mounted under the rear fuselage). The bomb fell in a completely normal manner, but could be steered left or right by the bomb aimer, using a special control installed at his position. To help him do this, the 'Azon' bomb generally was attached to a smoke flare. 'Azon' was intended for difficult 'linear' targets: viaducts and bridges.

The first 'Azon' mission conducted by *The Buck Rogers Boys* (as the rest of the 753rd called the specially-trained crews) was on 4th June to the bridge at Melun. 'Azon' had its successes but was generally regarded as a failure, particularly as it forced the 'Libs' down to lower altitudes and therefore increased their vulnerability. The last 'Azon' missions were flown by the 753rd in September 1944. 'Azon' can be regarded as the progenitor of today's so-called 'smart' bombs which have been used to devastating effect in precise bombing missions.

### Group Markings

White disc on upper starboard wing on olive drab aircraft with an insignia blue capital 'K' within the disc (on silver aircraft, the disc was black). A white disc was carried on vertical tails until May 1944 when tails were painted red with a white vertical stripe.

Squadron codes were grey on olive drab and black on silver aircraft, as follows:

| | |
|---|---|
| 752nd Squadron | '7V-' |
| 753rd Squadron | 'J4-' |
| 754th Squadron | 'Z5-' |
| 755th Squadron | 'J3-' |

The 458th used 'bar' (minus) signs with their individual call-letter, but not, apparently, to denote individual squadrons. Some aircraft also used the 'last three' of their serial number as an identifier, on the nose.

*Left:* **A 'GI' stands guard on an 'Azon' B-24 of the 753rd with the aerial array in the foreground. The specially-equipped aircraft were used for operational guided-bomb trials.**

*Below, centre:* **The 458th BG's *Bo* on one of the Group's first missions. The aircraft, B-24H-10-DT 41-28718, was allocated to the 752nd BS and was interned in Sweden on 29th April 1944, force-landing there after a raid on Berlin.**

*Bottom:* **In contrast to the heat of the journey from the USA, via Brazil and Africa, the 458th arrived in the depths of the English winter as evident in this early photograph of two of the Group's aircraft taxying through the snow at Horsham. Nearest the camera is B-24J-95-CO 42-100365 – *Battlin' Baby* of the 752nd BS.**

*Right:* ***Satan's Mate*****, B-24J-95-CO 42-100341 of the 753rd BS, 458th BG. It later became an 'Azon' aircraft and crashed in Holland on 11th July 1944 returning from a raid on Munich.**

*Below:* **The 458th holding a tight formation on one of its initial outings. The 'Z5' coded aircraft in the foreground are from the 754th.**

*Top:* **Seconds before touch down for B-24H-10-DT 41-28678 from the 458th BG's 755th BS. On 22nd March 1944 this aircraft crashed in Holland whilst returning from a mission to Berlin.**

*Centre:* **Tight formation; in the background is B-24H-15-FO 42-52441 *Last Card Louis* of the 755th, in the foreground is B-24H-15-FO 42-52335 *Admirable Little Character* of the 754th – note that the starboard outer is feathered.**

*Left:* ***The Cats*, B-24H-20-FO 42-94946, at Payerne, Switzerland. With the 458th BG's 754th BS, it force-landed with engine trouble during a mission to Neunkirchen on 27th May 1944.**

*Above:* **Former 'Azon' aircraft, B-24J-140-CO 42-110163, *Time's a' Wastin'* of the 458th BG's 753rd BS, begins its take-off run at Horsham.**

*Right:* **On 22nd April 1944, German intruders caused chaos when they attacked 2nd AD aircraft over their bases as they returned late and in darkness after a mission to Hamm. One of two 458th BG aircraft shot down was B-24J-95-CO 42-100357, from the 754th BS, which crashed near *The Bull* public house at Hellesdon, only a short distance from Horsham. Four of the crew managed to parachute to safety, but three others were killed in the crash. The pilot, Lt Charles W Stilson, was awarded the Silver Star for his vain efforts to save the stricken aircraft.**

*Below:* **B-24J-95-CO 42-100366 of the 754th BS, parked at a wet Horsham. The name *Mizpah* is an ancient Hebrew word which means 'the Lord watch between me and thee while we are absent from each other'.**

*Top left:* **Aircraft of the 753rd Bomb Squadron taxi out for the 24th December 1944 mission to Schönecken, led by 42-100408, a dragon-nosed B-24J-100-CO.**

*Below centre:* **Ready for take-off at Horsham before the group's 200th mission, to Berlin, on 26th February 1945, is B-24J-155-CO 44-40285 *Table Stuff*, from the 753rd BS.**

*Bottom:* **B-24J-140-CO 42-110141 *Breezy Lady* suffered a nosewheel failure after landing with the port inner propeller feathered. Formerly a 492nd BG aircraft, she flew with the 753rd Squadron and survived the war.**

*Above:* ***Gas House Mouse*****, B-24H-25-FO 42-95050 from the 458th BG's 752nd BS, parked at Manston, in Kent, after making a forced landing there due to damage sustained on a raid to Hanau on 11th December 1944. An Avro Lancaster is in the mid-background.**

*Right:* **752nd BS B-24J-105-CO 42-109812 with** ***Little Lambsy Divey*****, B-24J-100-CO 42-100407, in the background.**

*Below:* ***Nokkish*** **was salvaged at Horsham after running its port mainwheel into a ditch on 29th April 1944. B24H-10-CF, 41-29302, from the 752nd ('7V') Squadron, is call-letter 'P'.**

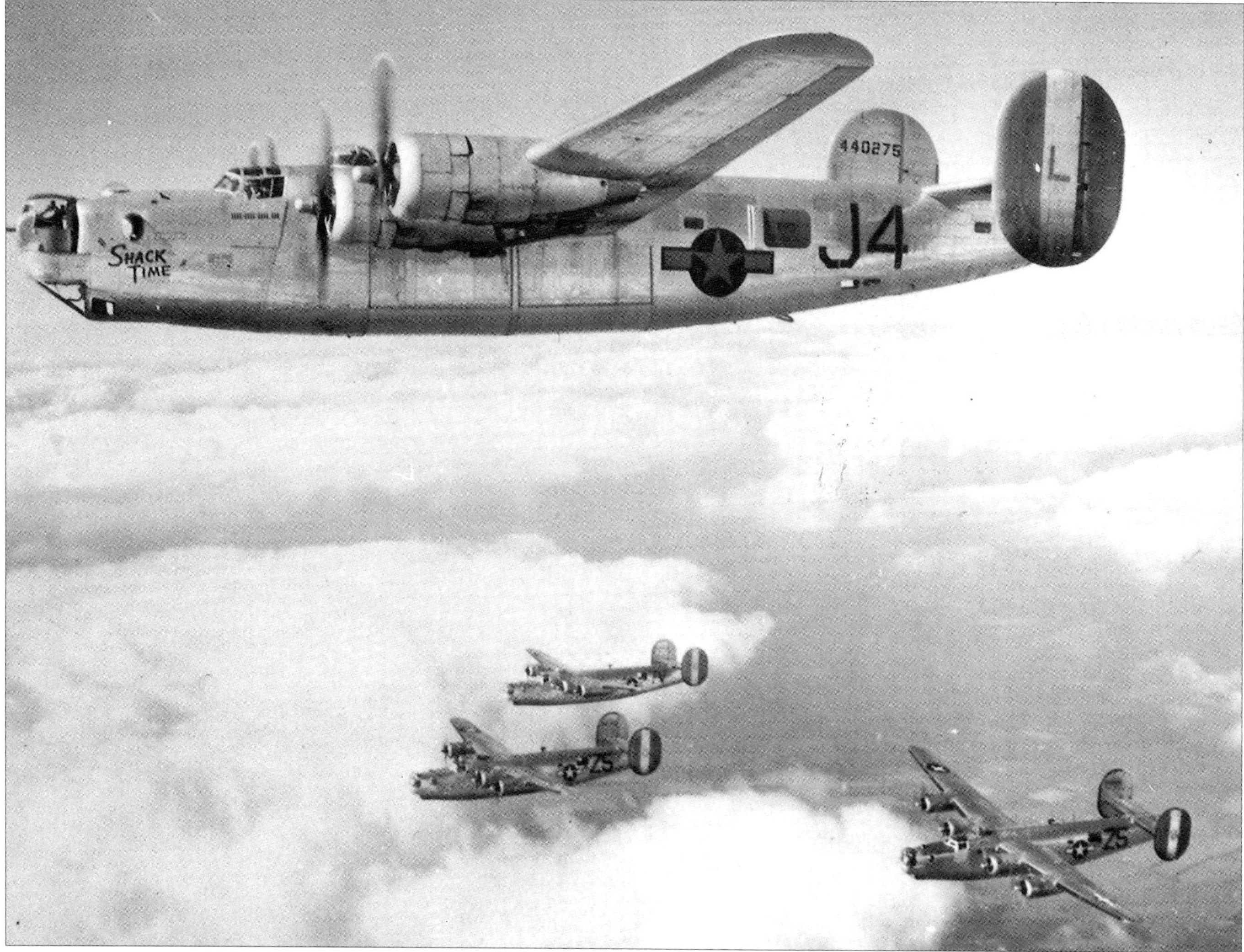


*Top:* ***Briney Marlin*****, B-24H-25-FO 42-95183 of the 755th BS, 458th BG.**

*Bottom:* **A mixed formation of 458th BG aircraft led by *Shack Time* of the 753rd BS. A B-24J-155-CO, 44-40275 was one of the ten original Liberators fitted for use as an 'Azon' aircraft. The aerials under the rear fuselage have been removed in this view.**

*Top:* ***The Shack*****, B-24J-160-CO 44-40298 of the 754th BS, 458th BG, an aircraft that originally flew with the 487th and 493rd BGs before the 3rd Air Division converted to Boeing B-17 Flying Fortresses.**

*Above:* **Bright winter sunshine helps disperse the early morning mist as 753rd BS aircraft taxi out for take-off from runway 05 at Horsham for a mission to Schönecken on 24th December 1944. Note the runway control caravan and the aircraft forming up overhead.**

**Nearest the camera is B-24J-1-FO 42-50555** ***Baby Shoes*** **(which also served with the 492nd). As a boy it was always the author's dream to live in one of the houses bordering the airfield, a wish probably not shared by the residents at the time!**

*Left:* **Tragedy struck on 14th January 1945 when B-24J-155-CO 44-40283 *Lassie Come Home,* of the 458th BG's 753rd BS, crashed in the back garden of a house at Mile Cross, Norwich. The aircraft had returned from a mission to Hallendorf with engine trouble and crashed on approach to Horsham, killing two children and eight of the nine-man crew.**

*Below, centre:* **Ground engineers test the engines of 755th BS B-24H-25-DT 42-51179 on its hardstand at Horsham St Faith.**

*Bottom:* ***Final Approach*, B-24H-15-FO 42-52457, ready for take-off at Horsham before the Group's 200th mission, to Berlin, on 26th February 1945. A 752nd BS veteran, it had done well over 100 missions before it was shot down by flak over the target of the day, Lechfeld airfield, on 9th April 1945.**

*Top:* **Pleasing flying portrait of *Silver Chief*, B-24J-150-CO 44-40201. One of the 492nd BG's original aircraft, it joined the 458th BG's 753rd BS when the former group disbanded. It is fitted with additional non-standard metal plating to the nose turret.**

*Bottom:* **Squadron codes were prominently displayed on 458th BG aircraft as shown by 754th BS B-24J-401-CF 42-50456 ('Z5'), which is in close company with B-24J-1-FO 42-95610 from the 752nd BS ('7V').**

*Top:* **B-24J-155-CO 44-40273 *Howling Banshee*, a former 'Azon' aircraft from the 753rd BS at Horsham, photographed in December 1944. The entire rear fuselage had just been replaced by the rear section from another damaged example by a repair crew from the 3rd Strategic Air Depot at Neaton, after *Howling Banshee* had been involved in a taxying accident.**

*Bottom:* **Colonel James Isbell, CO of the 458th BG, runs up the engine of *Ginny*, the Group's Thunderbolt formation monitor. This P-47D-25-RE (probably 42-26560, the serial unusually stencilled on the upper rear fuselage above the 'Star 'n Bar'), has its fin and rudder painted in the 458th's markings and carries the call-letter 'X'.**

## 466th BOMBARDMENT GROUP (H)
### *The Flying Deck*

The 466th Bomb Group arrived in England in early March 1944 and commenced operations later that month with a mission to Berlin on the 22nd. The Group went on to complete 232 missions flying the final one on 25th April 1945. Known as *The Flying Deck* (a frequently-used playing card analogy), the 466th released a total of 12,914 tons of bombs and claimed 29 enemy aircraft destroyed, 3 probables and 14 damaged.

### Group Markings

A circle containing a capital 'L' on the upper starboard wing (white on olive drab aircraft, black on silver machines). A white disc with dark blue 'L' on the vertical outer tail surfaces was used until May 1944 when outer tails painted red with white horizontal band. The Group adopted the practice of painting engine cowl rings in the squadron colours with the 784th Squadron using red, the 785th dark blue, the 786th yellow and the 787th white.

Squadron codes were grey on olive drab or black on silver aircraft, as follows:

| | |
|---|---|
| 784th Squadron | 'T9 -' |
| 785th Squadron | '2U -' |
| 786th Squadron | 'U8 -' |
| 787th Squadron | '6L -' |

The Group employed 'bar' and 'plus' signs with their call-letters, as follows:

| | |
|---|---|
| 784th Squadron | no sign |
| 785th Squadron | '+' after |
| 786th Squadron | 'bar' after |
| 787th Squadron | 'bar' below |

*Below:* **The 466th BG's *Jamaica?* lifts off from Attlebridge. A B-24H-10-DT (41-28746) from the 785th BS, *Jamaica?* was lost on a 'trucking' mission, ferrying gasoline to France, on 25th September 1944.**

*Bottom:* **On 13th April 1944 the 466th BG went to attack the air depot at Lechfeld, Germany, and had one loss, B-24H-15-FO 42-52567 of the 787th BS which force-landed at Dübendorf, Switzerland. The pilot, Lt N C Flynn, had obvious problems as can be seen by the feathered propeller on No.2 engine and the fresh oil stains on the lower fin and rudder.**

*Top:* **Another view of the 466th's *Jamaica?* On 15th June 1944 she force-landed on a fighter strip in Normandy after having been badly damaged by flak during a raid on Evreux airfield.**

*Above, centre:* ***Lady Lightning* (B-24H-15-FO 42-52597) of the 784th BS, being prepared for its next mission at the 466th BG's base at Attlebridge.**

*Bottom left:* **B-24H-15-CF 41-29387 *Snafu Snark* of the 785th BS, 466th BG, on its landing run at Attlebridge.**

*Top:* **The 466th's *The Falcon*, B-24H-25-FO 42-95248, from the 785th BS, which was destroyed in a crash-landing at Shipdham on 8th January 1945. Like most 466th BG aircraft *The Falcon* had coloured cowling rings, in this case blue, denoting squadron assignment.**

*Centre:* **During September 1944 several 2nd AD groups were involved in 'trucking' operations, flying gasoline and other supplies to airfields in France. A mixed line-up is headed by B-24H-30-CF 42-50438 *Miss Minooky* of the 466th BG's 786th BS.**

*Right:* **Landing gear failure for B-24J-401-CF 42-50488 of the 466th BG's 784th BS, upon return from a mission to Remagen on 2nd January 1945.**

*Top left:* **B-24J-145-CO 44-40093, *Lovely Lady's Avenger* from the 466th BG's 786th BS, was badly damaged by flak and fighters during a mission to Berlin on 21st June 1944. The pilot, Lt Leo Mower, just managed to get the aircraft to the Swedish coast where it crash-landed with all the crew surviving.**

*Top right:* **Hydraulic failure prompted these parachutes to be deployed from the waist windows of 466th BG B-24H-25-DT 42-51141 *Pegasus,* helping to slow it down on landing.**

*Centre and bottom:* **Snow and frost may make a nice picture but were certainly not welcomed by ground crew at Attlebridge. *Duffy's Tavern,* a 784th BS B-24J-10-FO is shown above while (centre) left to right are *Laden Maid Again* and an unnamed B-24J, both from the 786th BS, and the olive drab *Parson's Chariot*.**

*Top:* **Aircraft from the 466th BG's 785th BS led by *Fran*, B-24L-10-FO 44-49582 from the 784th BS. *Fran* is readily identified as a pathfinder aircraft, having a radome in place of the ball turret.**

*Bottom:* **Smoke markers and 500-pounders on their way down from a 466th BG formation, comprising mostly 787th BS ('6L') aircraft, with a lone 784th BS ('T9') example at top right.**

*Top left:* **B-24J-55-CF 44-10499 *Dixie* from the 785th Squadron. Happily *Dixie* survived the war.**

*Top right:* **The second *Parson's Chariot* to fly with the 446th was B-24M-10-FO 44-50699, assigned to the 784th Squadron.**

*Above, centre:* **B-24H-25-FO 42-95255 *Lady Luck* over mountainous terrain, probably Austria. *Lady* survived hostilities.**

*Bottom:* **The final version of the Liberator to fly with the 8th Air Force were the Ford-built 'Ms, this example being B-24M-5-FO 44-50490 of the 787th BS.**

## 467th BOMBARDMENT GROUP (H)
### *The Rackheath Aggies*

The 467th joined the 96th Combat Wing in mid-March 1944 and were based just north of Norwich, at Rackheath airfield, from where they took their name. They flew their first combat mission to Bourges airfield on 10th April 1944.

The 467th dropped a total of 13,333 tons of bombs during its 212 missions and had the best standards of bombing accuracy of any group in the 8th Air Force. It lost a total of 48 B-24s, and claimed six enemy aircraft destroyed with five damaged and two probables.

### Group Markings

A disc with a capital 'P' on the upper starboard wing (white on olive drab aircraft, black on silver machines). A similar disc with a capital 'P' was carried on the tail surfaces until May 1944, when tails were painted red with a white diagonal stripe.

Squadron codes were grey on olive drab aircraft, black on silver, as follows:

788th Squadron 'X7-'
789th Squadron '6A-'
790th Squadron 'Q2-'
791st Squadron '4Z-'

The Group employed 'bar' and 'plus' signs with their call-letters, as follows:

788th Squadron no sign
789th Squadron 'bar' above
790th Squadron 'bar' below
791st Squadron '+' after

*Top:* ***Tailwind*****, B-24H-15-CF 41-29368 from 467th BG's 789th BS, during a practice mission in April 1944.**

*Below:* **Still wearing the old style tail markings (and also note the call-letter 'N' with a bar below) is B-24H-20-CF 42-50354 –** ***Fickle Finger of Fate*** **from the 790th BS, after force-landing at Geneva, Switzerland, on 11th May 1944: the pilot was Lt William T Shoup.**

*Top:* **Two aircraft of the 467th BG's 790th BS during a practice mission in July 1944 over Somerleyton Park, with the coast near Gorleston in the background. Both are B-24H-15-CFs – 41-29408 and *Tangerine,* alias 41-29446, in the foreground.**

*Bottom:* ***Miss Fortune*, B-24H-15-FO 42-52559, from the 467th BG's 790th BS, which landed at Dübendorf with engine trouble on 12th July 1944.**

*Top:* **One of the most famous Liberators in the 2nd Air Division was the 467th BG's *Witchcraft*. A B-24H-15-FO (42-52534) from the 790th BS, it flew on the Group's first mission to Bourges, France, 10th April 1944 and on the next-to-last mission to Salzburg on 21st April 1945, a total of 130 trips without an abort.**

*Bottom:* **Flying gasoline and other supplies to airfields in France is B-24H-15-FO 42-52303 with the top-hatted gent nose-art in the foreground, also *Go Getter*. Both are from the 467th BG.**

*Left:* **The 467th BG's *Lil Peach*, B-24H-15-CF 41-29375, from the 791st BS, in unfamiliar surroundings as it taxies past the control tower at North Pickenham. Like many 467th BG aircraft it has a '9' painted on the inside of No.1 engine nacelle and would have a '3' in a similar position on the other outboard engine. This was to assist the top turret gunner in establishing the location of enemy aircraft using the 'clock' system.**

*Centre left:* **A perfect touch down for *Three Star Special*, B-24H-20-FO 42-94986, of the 788th BS. This former 492nd BG aircraft had the last three numbers of the serial painted on the nose, a practice adopted by the 467th BG towards the end of 1944.**

*Bottom:* ***Witchcraft* and the ground crew that kept her flying, pause for a one-minute silence on Memorial Day, amid the clutter needed to keep a B-24 fully operational.**

*Opposite page:*

*Top:* **Liberators of the 790th BS on their hardstands at Rackheath near Dakenham Hall Farm. The aircraft on the extreme right is *Witchcraft*.**

*Bottom:* ***Perils of Pauline* from the 467th's 790th BS during a practice mission on 10th June 1944. A B-24H-25-FO (42-95162), the aircraft was lost during a mission to Brunswick on 5th August 1944.**

Q2
Q2

295162
Q2

*Top:* **The scene at Rackheath airfield with *Wolves Inc*, B-24H-20-DT 41-28981 of the 791st BS, on its hardstand near the Salhouse road railway crossing.**

*Bottom:* ***Angel* comes into land at the 467th BG's base at Rackheath. B-24H-25-FO 42-95057 flew with the 790th BS. Note the 'last three' applied to the nose over the name, and her two companions downwind.**

*Opposite page, top:* **Pathfinder B-24L-10-FO 44-49591 from the 467th BG's 791st BS, touches down at Rackheath.**

*Opposite page, bottom:* **B-24J-1-DT 42-51282 of the 791st BS 467th BG.**

591
4Z

1282
4Z
282

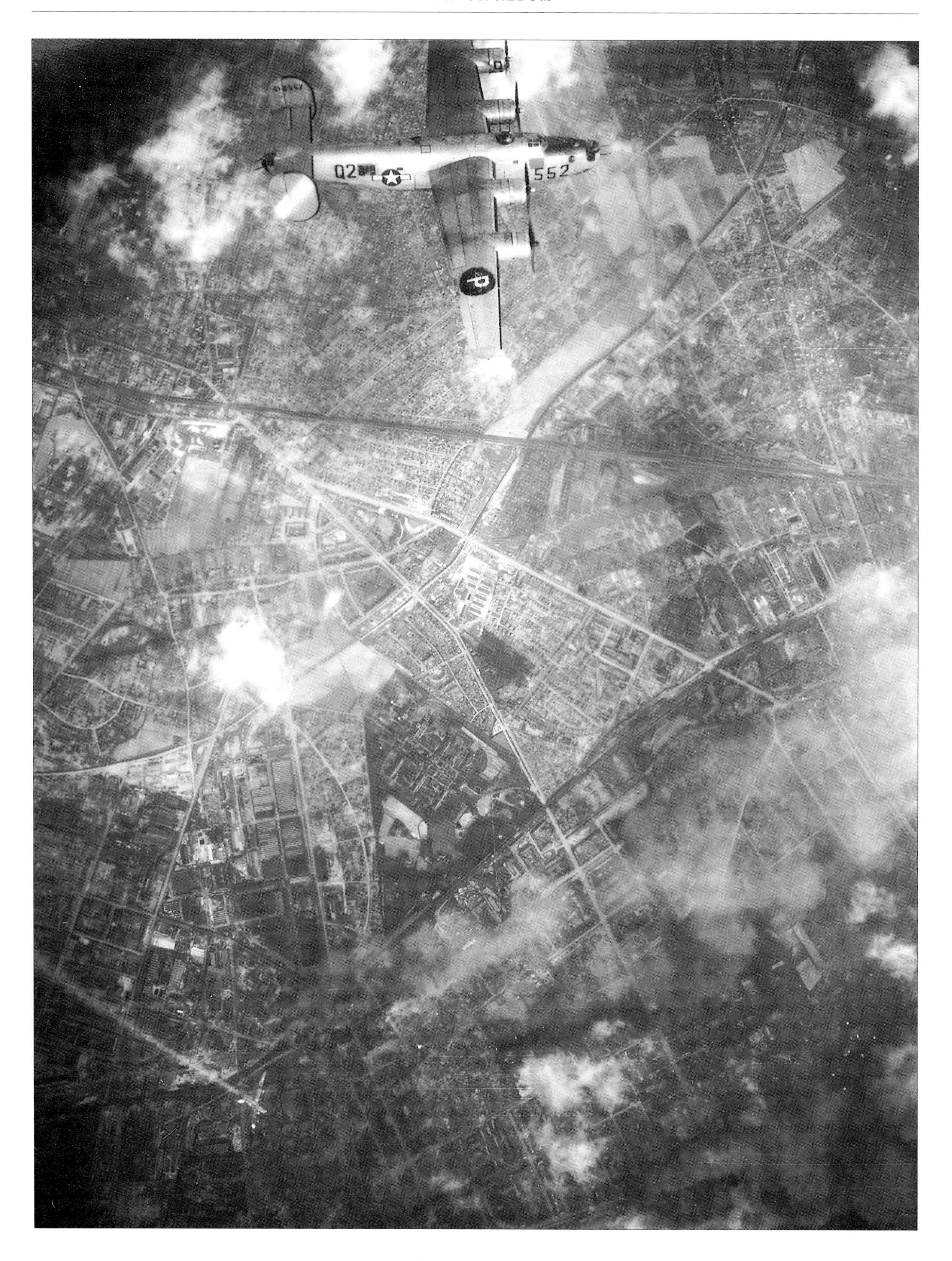
Q2
552
P

*Opposite page:*

**B-24J-60-CF 44-10552 from the 467th BG's 790th BS high over Berlin on 18th March 1945. In the bottom left of the picture B-24H-15-FO 42-52546 *Southern Clipper* can be seen going down on fire, a victim of the city's flak.**

*This page:*

*Top:* **B-24H-25-FO 42-95224 *Lonely Heart* from the 467th BG was involved in a mid-air collision during a practice mission on 22nd August 1944, in which the nose was very badly damaged. *Heart* successfully returned to Rackheath and was later flown to Watton for the attentions of the 3rd Strategic Air Depot at Neaton with timber bracing fitted and a tarpaulin over the nose. A new nose section was grafted on and the aircraft returned to service.**

*Centre right:* **B-24L-10-FO 44-49610 from the 791st BS, 467th BG, stuck in the mud after a landing accident on 24th March 1945.**

*Bottom:* **Just seconds after bomb release, two 789th BS aircraft on the 467th BG's mission to Lechfeld air depot on 9th April 1945. *Massillon Tiger*, B-24J-55-CF 44-10488 is nearest.**

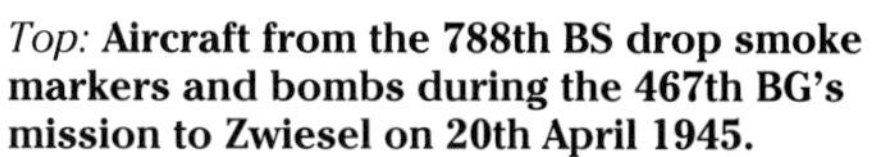

*Top:* **Aircraft from the 788th BS drop smoke markers and bombs during the 467th BG's mission to Zwiesel on 20th April 1945.**

*Left:* **B-24H-15-CF 41-29348 almost had its nose section severed when the port outer prop flew off during a crash-landing at Woodbridge on return from the low level supply mission to Holland on 18th September 1944. The aircraft was on loan to the 491st BG at the time.**

*Lower left:* ***Baffling Brat*, B-24H-15-FO 42-52512 from the 790th. She was lost on the Munich mission on 12th July 1944.**

*Bottom left:* **Touching down at Rackheath late in the war, B-24J-65-CF 44-10601 *Rosalyn* survived hostilities.**

*Opposite page:*

*Top:* **Almost new B-24H-25-FO 42-95273 from Rackheath's 790th Squadron releases 12 x 500lb bombs a split second before its three companions in the background. The latter include *Witchcraft* to the right and *Snooper* in front.**

*Bottom:* ***Little Pete 2*, one of the 467th BG's 'hack' Thunderbolts. This machine (probably P-47D-25-RE 42-26393), carries the Group insignia on the nose and the red and white tail colours, and was often flown by the CO, Colonel Shower, as a monitor aircraft during group assembly.**

Q2

393

*Left and immediately below:* **Before and after the spots. Two views of *First Sergeant*, the 458th BG's original assembly ship which was destroyed by fire after a flare accident at Horsham in late May 1944. A B-24D-30-CO, 42-40127 previously flew with the 93rd BG as *Thar She Blows* and was a veteran of the Ploesti mission. Her spots were red and blue on the front half of the fuselage and red and yellow on the rear portion.**

*Left, below, and opposite page top:* **Three views of the 458th BG's second assembly ship, *Spotted Ape*, B-24H-20-DT 41-28967, a former 754th BS aircraft.**

*Right:* **This proved to be the end of the road for the *Spotted Ape*, the 458th's second assembly ship, after crash-landing at Horsham in early March 1945.**

*Below:* **The 466th BG's silver and red assembly ship, B-24D-20-CO 41-24109, formerly flew with the 44th and 93rd BG's as *Ready and Willing* and was eventually scrapped at Watton in May 1945.**

*Left and immediately below:* **The 467th's assembly ship, *Pete the POM Inspector*, B-24D-53-CO 42-40370, flew previously with the 44th BG and the 389th as *Heaven Can Wait* and was written-off after a landing accident at Rackheath in October 1944.**

*Bottom:* **The replacement was *Pete the POM Inspector 2nd,* Although resembling a 'D model, *Pete the POM Inspector 2nd* was 41-29393, the former *Shoo Shoo Baby*, a B-24H-15-CF with a 'D 'glass-house' grafted on to the nose section. Both *Petes* were painted black overall with yellow discs outlined in red.**

**458th BOMBARDMENT GROUP:**

***Liberty Lib*, B-24H-10-CF 41-29303 of the 752nd BS.**

***Little Lambsy Divey*, B-24J-100-CO 42-100407 of the 752nd BS.**

***Belle of Boston*, B-24H-15-FO 42-52404 of the 754th BS. Crashed at Frettenham after take-off for the Brunswick mission, 8th May 1944.**

***Satan's Mate*, B-24J-95-CO 42-100341 of the 753rd BS.**

***Rhapsody in Junk*, B-24H-10-DT 41-28733 of 753rd BS.**

***Flak Magnet*, B-24H-10-CF 41-29273 of the 753rd BS. *Flak Magnet* turned out to be all too appropriate; it was hit by flak over the target on 22nd April 1944 on a mission to Hamm.**

**458th BOMBARDMENT GROUP:**

***Bomb Totin' Mama*, B-24H-10-CF 41-29295 of the 754th BS was shot down by fighters on 9th April 1944 on a mission to Tutow.**

***Meat Around the Corner*, B-24H-10-DT 41-28738 of the 754th BS. It crashed in Switzerland on 11th May 1944 on a mission to Epinal.**

***Shack Time*, B-24J-155-CO 44-40275 was one of the ten original Liberators fitted for use as an 'Azon' aircraft.**

***Paddlefoot*, B-24H-10-DT 41-28719 of the 755th BS, with an original method of noting the mission tallies.**

***Lassie Come Home*, B-24J-155-CO 44-40283, of the 753rd BS.**

***Nokkish*, B-24H-10-CF 41-29302 of the 458th. The small projection above the second 'K' in the name is the navigator's drift sight.**

**458th BOMBARDMENT GROUP:**

***Final Approach*, B-24H-15-FO 42-52457 of the 752nd BS.**

**466th BOMBARDMENT GROUP:**

***Lady Lightning*, B-24H-15-FO 42-52597 of the 784th BS. The *Lady* was lost on 15th August 1944 on a mission to Vechta.**

***Jamaica ?*, B-24H-10-DT 41-28746 port and starboard sides. Note the names and home states neatly stencilled under the crew positions.**

***The Mad Monk*, B-24H-15-CF 41-29402 of the 786th BS. It crash-landed at Swanton Morley after take-off, 25th July 1944.**

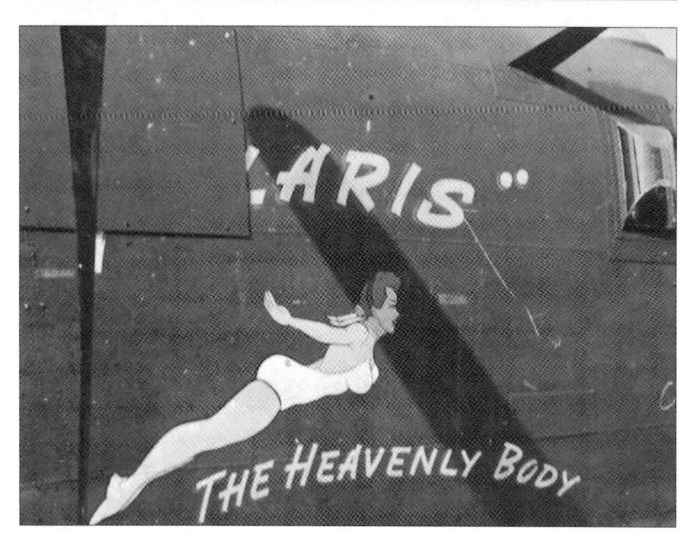


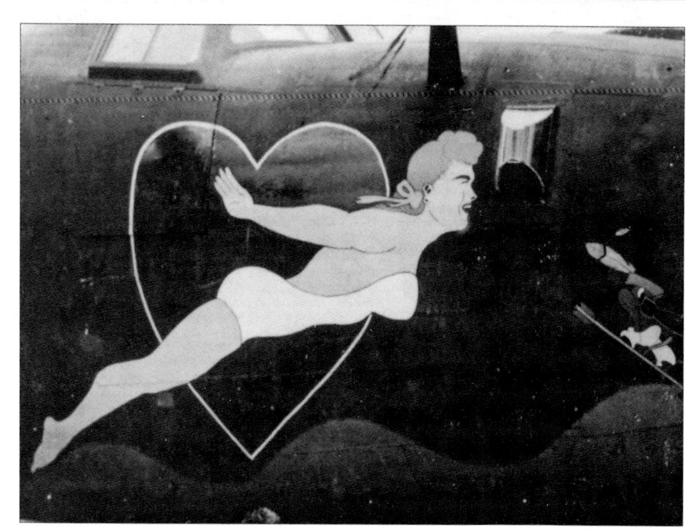

**466th BOMBARDMENT GROUP:**

***Playboy***, **B-24H-15-CF 41-29399 of the 784th BS. It crash-landed in Holland after a raid on Berlin on 29th April 1944.**

***Gallopin' Ghost***, **B-24H-15-CF 41-29439 of the 787th BS, crashed on a 'trucking' mission on 29th September 1944.**

***Polaris, The Heavenly Body***, **B-24H-15-CF 41-29384, of the 787th BS, crash-landed at Attlebridge on return from Neunkirchen on 27th May 1944.**

***Reliable Babe***, **B-24H-15-FO 42-52527 of the 786th BS, was salvaged at Woodbridge, August 1944.**

***Bird Dog***, **B-24H-25-FO 42-95084 of the 784th BS, crashed just after take-off at East Tunstall, Norfolk on a mission to Saarbrücken on 13th July 1944.**

***Queen of Hearts***, **B-24H-15-FO 42-52511 of the 786th BS, crash-landed at New Romney, Kent, after a mission to a V-weapons site on 17th July 1944.**

**466th BOMBARDMENT GROUP:**

**Crew members' home states proudly displayed near their flight stations on *Little Lulu*, B-24H-15-CF 41-29391, of the 787th BS.**

***Betta Duck*, B-24J-165-CO 44-40454, which flew for seven months with the 785th Squadron at Attlebridge after transferring from the 34th Bomb Group at Mendlesham.**

***Dixie*, B-24J-55-CF 44-10499 from the 785th Squadron.**

**On 1st September 1944 *Liberty Belle*, B-24H-25-DT 42-51134, from the 784th BS, should have been deputy lead for the 458th BG on a mission to Pfaffenhoffen. However it crashed on take-off from Horsham, killing all 12 crew.**

***The Falcon*, B-24H-25-FO 42-95248 from the 785th BS.**

**466th BOMBARDMENT GROUP:**

***Let 'Er Rip*, B-24M-5-FO 44-50548 of the 785th BS.**

***Laden Maid*, B-24H-15-FO 42-52560 of the 786th BS was salvaged December 1944.**

***Damifino*, B-24J-401-CF 42-50465 of the 784th BS.**

***Crow's Nest*, B-24H-20-FO 42-95010 of the 786th BS, crash-landed near Brussels after raid on Gelsenkirchen, 25th October 1944.**

***Belle*, B-24H-20-DT 42-51099 of the 785th BS.**

***Biff Bam*, B-24H-25-FO 42-95283, of the 785th BS was salvaged 29th May 1945.**

**467th BOMBARDMENT GROUP:**

***Tangerine*, B-24H-15-CF 41-29446 of the 790th BS.**

***Miss Fortune*, B-24H-15-FO 42-52559 of the 790th BS.**

**Striking nose-art on B-24H-15-CF 41-29385. *Double Trouble* flew with both the 791st and 789th Squadrons and saw out the war.**

***Snooper*, B-24H-15-FO 42-52571 of the 790th BS.**

***Lucky 'Leven*, B-24J-20-FO 44-48820, a 791st BS PFF aircraft.**

***Witchcraft*, B-24H-15-FO 42-52534 from the 790th BS proudly showing its 130 trips without an abort.**

**467th BOMBARDMENT GROUP:**

**Simple effective nose-art on B-24H-15-FO 42-52303 of the 791st BS.**

***Super Wolf*, B-24H-25-FO 42-95080 of the 791st BS. It was lost on the 16th February 1945 mission to Osnabrück.**

***Rosalyn*, B-24J-65-CF 44-10601 of the 788th BS.**

***Perils of Pauline*, B-24H-25-FO 42-95162 of the 467th's 790th BS.**

***Wabbit*, B-24H-15-FO 42-52623 of the 789th BS.**

***Prowler*, B-24J-140-CO 42-110171 of the 790th BS, previously with the 491st BG, was salvaged at Rackheath in June 1945.**

Appendix A

# 2nd AD
# Nose Art Reprise

**445th BG: 701st BS, *The Grim Reaper*, B-24J-100-CO 42-100404.**

**448th BG: *Piccadilly Lilly*, B-24H-20-CF 42-50341 of the 715th BS. She was lost on the low level supply mission to Wesel on 24th March 1945.**

**448th BG: *Squat 'N Droppit*, B-24H-10-DT 41-28710.**

**448th BG: 712th BS, *4-F*, B-24J-1-FO 42-95527.**

**448th BG: *The Commanche*, B-24H-5-CF 42-64447 of the 714th BS, lost on a mission to Frankfurt when hit by flak over Northern France.**

**448th BG: *Sturgeon*, B-24J-130-CO 42-110066 of the 715th BS, she survived the war.**

**466th BG: 753rd BS, *Times A' Wastin'*, B-24 J-1-FO (Not the same as 458th AC).**

**489th BG: *Bomb Baby*, B-24H-20-FO 42-94829.**

**489th BG: *Cover Girl*, B-24H-20-FO 42-94945.**

**489th BG: 844th BS, *Fords Folly*, B-24H-20-FO 42-94842.**

**489th BG: *Pin Up Girl*, B-24H-20-FO 42-94941.**

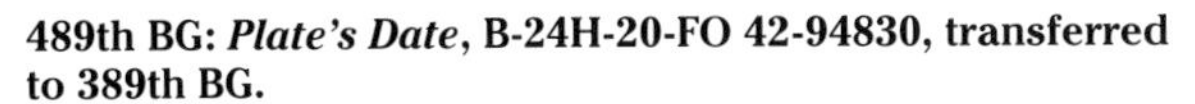
489th BG: *Plate's Date*, B-24H-20-FO 42-94830, transferred to 389th BG.

489th BG: 845th BS, *The Sharon D*, B-24H-15-FO 42-94759.

489th BG: 846th BS, *Slick Chick*, B-24H-25-CF 42-50388.

489th BG: *Tiger's Revenge*, B-24H-20-FO 42-94816.

491st BG: *The Little Gramper*, B-24D-90-CO 42-40722, assembly ship. Colour was overall yellow with red spots.

491st BG: 852nd BS, *Tung Hoi*, B-24J-150-CO 44-40230.

492nd BG: 857th, *Silver Chief*, B-24J-150-CO 44-40201.

Left: **The full nose of 2nd CBW, 389th BG B-24H-25-FO 42-95026 *Yankee Rebel*. Note the 14 bomb tallies, three of which have a diagonal line through them. *Rebel* succumbed to flak damage on 25th July 1944.**

Centre left: ***The Flying Jackass*, B-24J-150-CO 44-40239 of the 14th CBW's 491st BW, 853rd BS. It was destroyed in a ground accident at Manston on 25th March 1945.**

Bottom left: ***Rugged But Right*, B-24H-20-FO 42-94953 formerly with the 490th BG, she flew with the 448th's 715th BS at Seething and survived the war.**

Appendix B

# 2nd Air Division Colour

A series of paintings and side-view illustrations by the author.

Above: ***The Little Gramper*, B-24D-90-CO 42-40722 of the 2nd CBW's 389th BG, 566th BS.**

Below: ***Tubarão*, B-24J-145-CO of the 14th CBW's 491st BG, 854th BS**

*Screamin' Mimi*, B-24D-120-CO 42-40997 of the 2nd CBW's 389th BG, 564th BS, summer 1943.

*El Flako*, B-24H-10-CF 42-64469 of the 2nd CBW's 453rd BG, 732nd BS, autumn 1944.

*Will-er Run ?*, B-24H-1-FO 42-7526 of the 2nd CBW's 445th BG, 702nd BS, summer 1944.

*Princess Konocti*, B-24J-80-CO 42-100190 of the 2nd CBW, 389th BG, 566th BS, early summer 1944.

*Whiskey Jingles*, B-24H-25-DT 42-51114 of the 2nd CBW's 453rd BG, 733rd BS, winter 1944.

*Asbestos Alice*, B-24M-5-FO 44-50525 of the 2nd CBW's 445th BG, 700th BS, early 1945.

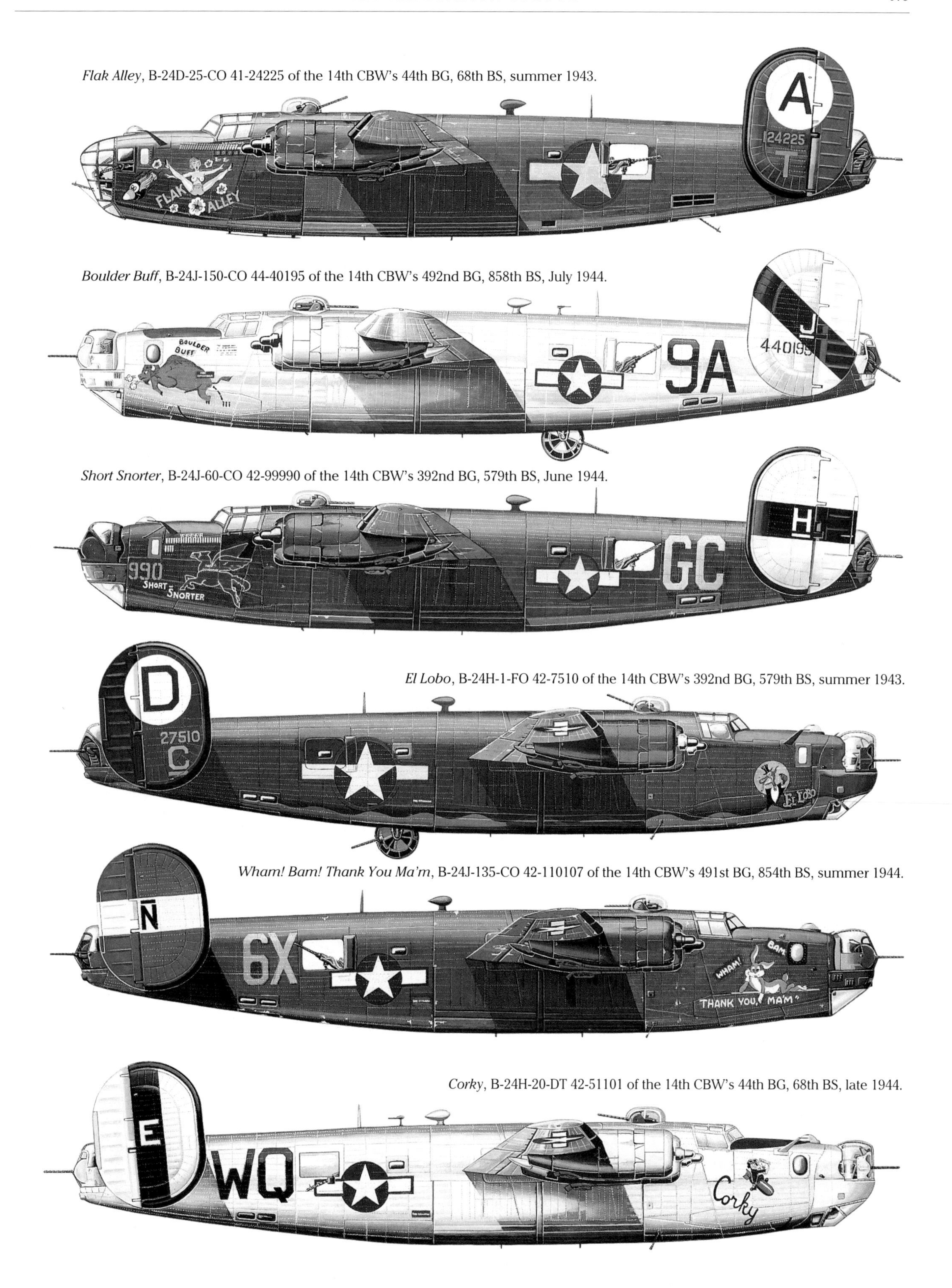


*Flak Alley*, B-24D-25-CO 41-24225 of the 14th CBW's 44th BG, 68th BS, summer 1943.

*Boulder Buff*, B-24J-150-CO 44-40195 of the 14th CBW's 492nd BG, 858th BS, July 1944.

*Short Snorter*, B-24J-60-CO 42-99990 of the 14th CBW's 392nd BG, 579th BS, June 1944.

*El Lobo*, B-24H-1-FO 42-7510 of the 14th CBW's 392nd BG, 579th BS, summer 1943.

*Wham! Bam! Thank You Ma'm*, B-24J-135-CO 42-110107 of the 14th CBW's 491st BG, 854th BS, summer 1944.

*Corky*, B-24H-20-DT 42-51101 of the 14th CBW's 44th BG, 68th BS, late 1944.

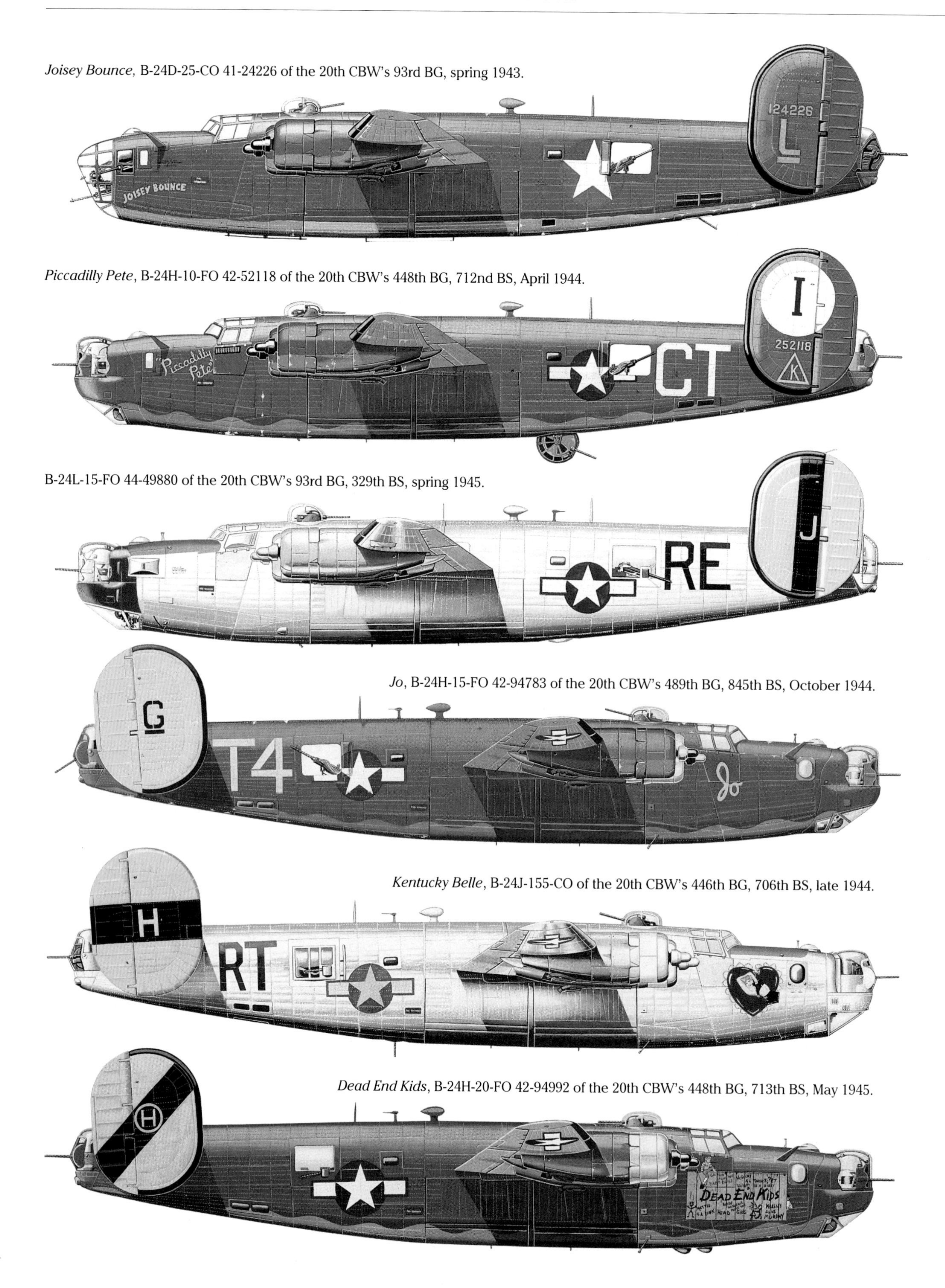


*Joisey Bounce*, B-24D-25-CO 41-24226 of the 20th CBW's 93rd BG, spring 1943.

*Piccadilly Pete*, B-24H-10-FO 42-52118 of the 20th CBW's 448th BG, 712nd BS, April 1944.

B-24L-15-FO 44-49880 of the 20th CBW's 93rd BG, 329th BS, spring 1945.

*Jo*, B-24H-15-FO 42-94783 of the 20th CBW's 489th BG, 845th BS, October 1944.

*Kentucky Belle*, B-24J-155-CO of the 20th CBW's 446th BG, 706th BS, late 1944.

*Dead End Kids*, B-24H-20-FO 42-94992 of the 20th CBW's 448th BG, 713th BS, May 1945.

*Lazy Lou*, **B-24H-1-FO of the 20th CBW's 446th BG, 706th BS.**

**_Duffy's Tavern_, a B-24J-10-FO of the 96th CBW's 466th BG, 784th BS.**

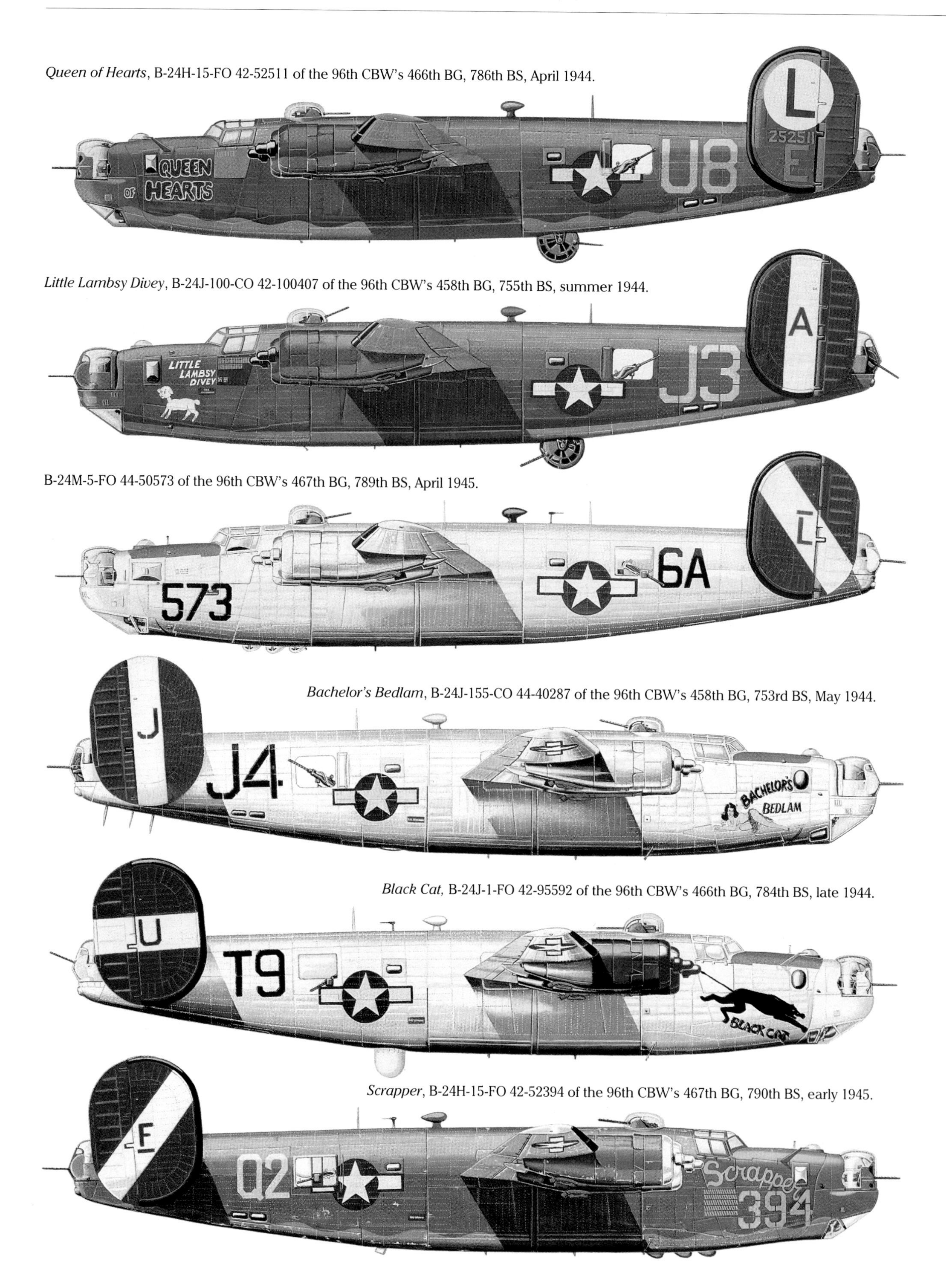


*Queen of Hearts*, B-24H-15-FO 42-52511 of the 96th CBW's 466th BG, 786th BS, April 1944.

*Little Lambsy Divey*, B-24J-100-CO 42-100407 of the 96th CBW's 458th BG, 755th BS, summer 1944.

B-24M-5-FO 44-50573 of the 96th CBW's 467th BG, 789th BS, April 1945.

*Bachelor's Bedlam*, B-24J-155-CO 44-40287 of the 96th CBW's 458th BG, 753rd BS, May 1944.

*Black Cat,* B-24J-1-FO 42-95592 of the 96th CBW's 466th BG, 784th BS, late 1944.

*Scrapper*, B-24H-15-FO 42-52394 of the 96th CBW's 467th BG, 790th BS, early 1945.

*Right and below, centre:* **Lil Cookie, the 489th BG's yellow polka-dotted B-24H-1-FO 42-7552 assembly ship. Also shown is the modified rear section carrying the cruciform signal lamp array.**

*Bottom:* **In late 1973, the 2nd Air Division returned to the skies of East Anglia. Chino, California-based Yesterday's Air Force acquired former Indian Air Force B-24J-95-CF HE771 (ex-RAF Mk.VII KH401 and built as 44-44272) and placed it on the US civil register as N94459. The 'Lib' was ferried from Poona to the Imperial War Museum airfield at Duxford, Cambridge-shire, arriving on 28th October of that year. At Duxford it was prepared for its new life and given the markings of B-24J-1-FO 42-50551 *Delectable Doris,* 'RR-R+' of the Hethel-based 566th BS, 389th BG. (See page 40 for the real *Doris*.) On 11th September 1975 the Liberator departed Prestwick, Scotland en route to its new home in the USA and today is part of the Fantasy of Flight collection at Polk City, Florida.**
*Ken Ellis collection*

*Advertisement*

## We hope you enjoyed this book . . .

Aerofax and Midland Publishing titles are edited and designed by an experienced and enthusiastic trans-Atlantic team of specialists.

Further titles are in preparation but we always welcome ideas from authors or readers for books they would like to see published.

In addition, our associate company, Midland Counties Publications, offers an exceptionally wide range of aviation, spaceflight, astronomy, military, naval and transport books and videos for sale by mail-order around the world.

For a copy of the appropriate catalogue, or to order further copies of this book, and any of the titles mentioned on this or the facing page, please write, telephone, fax or e-mail to:

**Midland Counties Publications**
Unit 3 Maizefield,
Hinckley, Leics, LE10 1YF, England

Tel: (+44) 01455 233 747
Fax: (+44) 01455 233 737
E-mail: midlandbooks@compuserve.com

US distribution by Specialty Press – see page 2.

**OKB SUKHOI**
A history of the design bureau and its aircraft

Vladimir Antonov et al, with Jay Miller

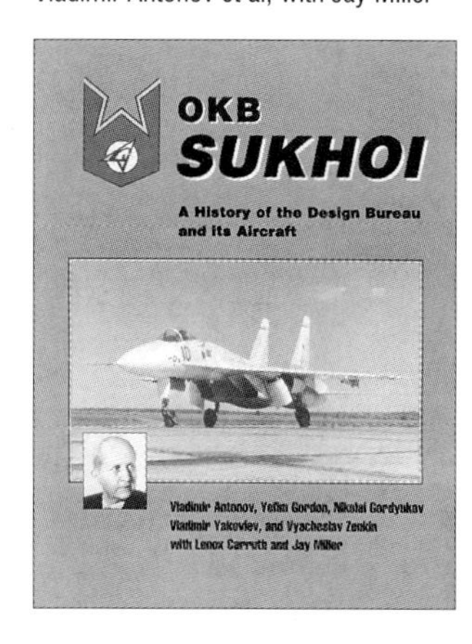


A team of authors have thoroughly documented the products of this famous Soviet aircraft design bureau, thanks to extensive access to the company records and photo files. A huge amount of unpublished information and illustrations are included. Each aircraft type is reviewed in detail, also prototypes, testbeds and projects, some of which never saw the light of day. Appendices detail test pilots and major personalities.

Hardback, 280 x 216 mm, 296pp
645 photos/illusts plus 23 in colour and 104 3-views and line drawings
1 85780 012 5 **£29.95/US $49.95**

**OKB MiG**
A history of the design bureau and its aircraft

Piotr Butowski, Jay Miller

Beginning with a comprehensive overview of Soviet military aviation, the text methodically moves from the births of Mikoyan and Gurevich through to the founding of the MiG design bureau during 1939, its war years, and the period of greatest importance, beginning with the advent of the MiG-15 and the Korean War and continuing via the MiG-17, -19, -21, -23, -25 and -27 to the MiG-29 and MiG-31 era. A highly acclaimed work.

Hardback, 280 x 216 mm, 248pp
800 photographs, over 100 drawings
0 904597 80 6 **£24.95/US $39.95**

**LOCKHEED MARTIN'S SKUNK WORKS**
The First Fifty Years (Revised Edition)

Jay Miller

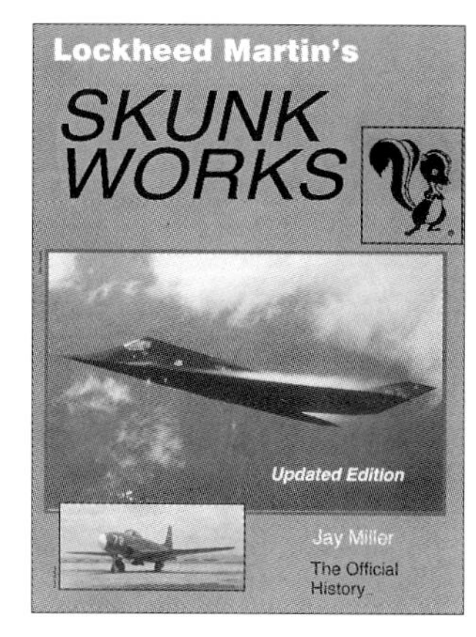


An updated edition of the original 1994 book – written with the co-operation of Lockheed Martin's Advanced Development Company. In a major 'pulling back' of the veil of secrecy, official histories of such products as the P80, RB-69, T-33, F-94, F-104 and CL-400, right the way through to the U-2, A-12, D-21, SR-71, and F-117, are finally brought to light.

This is the closest thing yet to a definitive history of this most enigmatic aircraft design and production facility.

Softback, 305 x 229 mm, 216 pages
479 b/w and 28 colour photos
1 85780 037 0 **£19.95/US $29.95**

**US MILITARY AIRCRAFT DESIGNATIONS & SERIALS 1909 to 1979**

John M Andrade

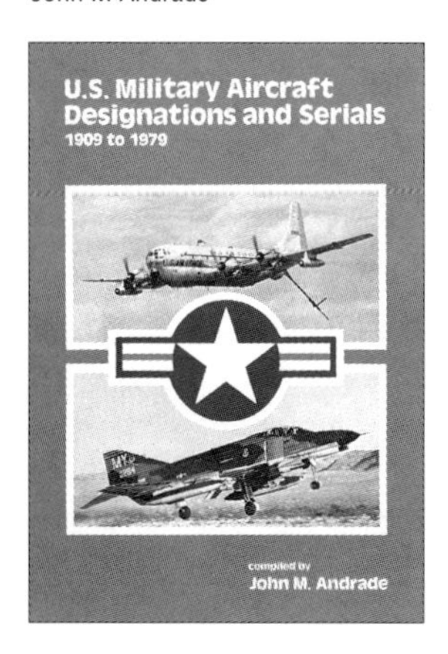


A straightforward reprint of this famous survey of the aircraft used by the United States Air Force, Army, Navy, Marines and other military and quasi-military services from 1909 thru' to 1979. It begins with an explanation of the various Mission Design Systems used over the years, and works through each individual designation, giving the aircraft types, manufacturers, names, quantities built, block numbers, variant differences, aircraft serial blocks, construction numbers and other details. Includes useful appendices.

Softback, 210 x 148 mm, 252 pages
0 904597 22 9 **£12.95 / $21.95**

**LUFTWAFFE SECRET PROJECTS**
Fighters 1939-1945

Walter Schick & Ingolf Meyer

With access to much previously unpublished information the authors bring to life futuristic shapes that might have terrorised the Allies had the war gone beyond 1945 using full colour action illustrations in contemporary unit markings and performance data tables. Careful comparison with later Allied and Soviet aircraft show the legacy handed on, right up to today's stealth aircraft. This first English-language edition benefits from author revisions and 20% additional information and illustrations.

Hardback, 282 x 213 mm, 176 pages
95 colour views, 160 drwgs, 30 photos
1 85780 052 4 **£29.95 / $44.95**

**ROYAL AIR FORCE BOMBER COMMAND LOSSES of the SECOND WORLD WAR**

W R Chorley

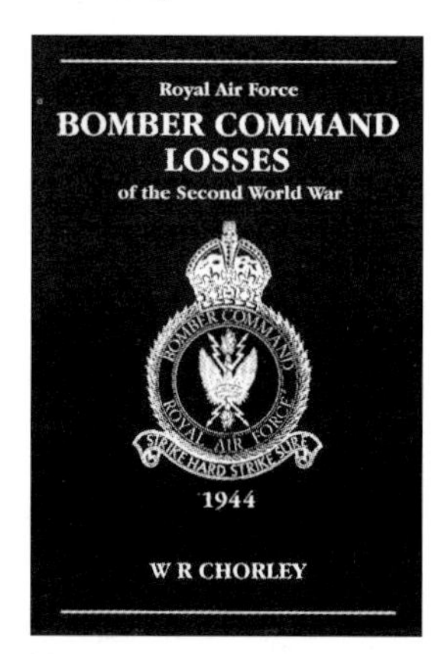


A series to cover the whole war, day-by-day, identifying units, aircraft, crews and the circumstances behind each European Theatre loss. Appendices include loss totals by group, squadron and aircraft type for each year; bases by group, bomber OTU losses by unit and type, PoWs, escapers etc. This series makes an ideal complement to *Bomber Command War Diaries.*

Available in 234 x 156mm, softback:
Vol 1-1939-40: 1,217 a/c, 160pp, **£9.95**
Vol 2-1941: 1,515 a/c, 224pp, **£12.95**
Vol 3-1942: 2,035 a/c, 318pp, **£15.95**
Vol 4-1943: 3,100 a/c, 494pp, **£18.95**
Vol 5-1944: 3,537 a/c, 576pp, **£19.95**

**THE BOMBER COMMAND WAR DIARIES** – An Operational Reference Book: 1939-45

Martin Middlebrook & Chris Everitt

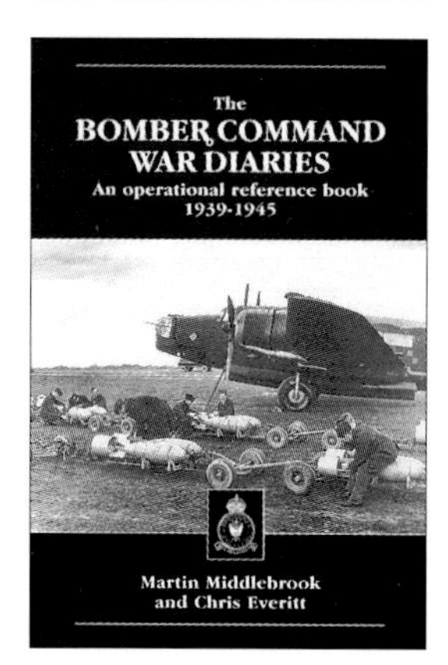


Provides a concisely-worded day-by-day review of each raid . Operational statistics provide unit and group sorties against aircraft lost – which range from 1% through to 18%. Copiously indexed, this is a balanced testament to Bomber Command, its men and rationale. This latest Midland Publishing edition includes minor amendments and new observations, but essentially *War Diaries* continues to be what it has always been, an icon in aviation publishing – the essential classic.

Softback, 234 x 156 mm, 808 pages
65 b/w photographs Available
1 85780 033 8 **£19.95 / $32.95**

In 1982, American author Jay Miller published his first major book, the 'AeroGraph' on the F-16. Since then there has been a steady flow of widely acclaimed books from the Aerofax line.

After many years acting as European distributors, Midland Publishing Limited acquired the rights to the Aerofax name and have since commissioned many new titles for the series. Some will continue to be produced for Midland by Jay Miller in the USA, others will be originated by a talented team of internationally known authors.

The previous categories of AeroGraph, DataGraph, MiniGraph, and Extra are no longer used; all new titles are simply published as 'Aerofax' books.

These softback volumes are full of authoritative text, detailed photographs, plus line drawings. They also contain some colour, and cockpits, control panels and other interior detail are well illustrated in most instances.

Some of the more recent titles are outlined alongside, whilst a listing of the others in the series that are still in print, plus details of newly announced titles, is available upon request.

The first two new-style 'Aerofax' titles were updated 'Extras', namely:

**Lockheed-Martin F-117** (Jay Miller)
1 85780 038 9 **£7.95/ US $12.95**

**Northrop B-2 Spirit** (Jay Miller)
1 85780 039 7 **£7.95/ US $12.95**

**Aerofax**
**CONVAIR B-58 HUSTLER**
The World's First Supersonic Bomber

Jay Miller

Convair B-58 Hustler
The world's first supersonic bomber

Instantly recognisable with its delta wing and 'coke bottle' area-ruled fuselage the B-58 was put into production for the US Air Force in the 1950s.

First published, in 1985, this revised edition, which takes a retrospective in-depth look at this significant aircraft, from design studies, through development and comparatively short service life to, and beyond retirement, includes yet more amazing material, and 80 new illustrations.

Softback, 280 x 216 mm, 152 pages
415 b/w, 14 colour, 100 line illusts.
1 85780 058 3 **£16.95/ US $27.95**

**Aerofax**
**GRUMMAN F-14 TOMCAT**
Leading US Navy Fleet Fighter

Dennis R Jenkins

Grumman F-14 Tomcat
US Navy Fleet Defense Fighter

Aerofax

Entering US Navy service in 1972, the Tomcat is still one of the classic jet fighters of all time. It remains a formidable weapon system and is still in widespread frontline use with America's carrier air wings.

This work describes all variants, including the so-called 'Bombcat' attack version and the very capable F-14D. Colour schemes, aircraft production details, squadrons and markings, are all covered, also close-up details of cockpits and weaponry.

Softback, 280 x 216 mm, 88 pages
151 b/w, 39 colour, 22 line illustrations
1 85780 063 X **£12.95 / US $21.95**

**Aerofax**
**BOEING KC-135**
More Than Just a Tanker

Robert S Hoskins III

Boeing KC-135 Stratotanker
More than just a Tanker

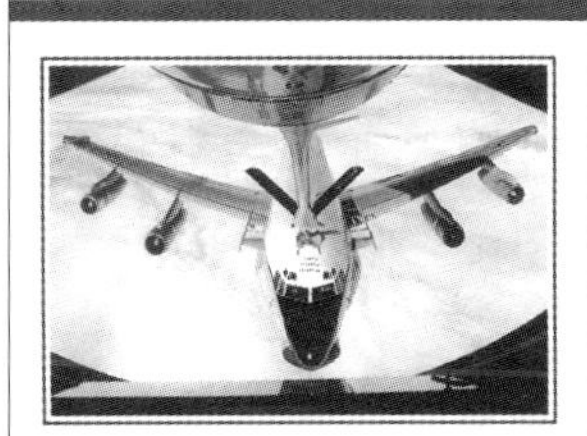

Robert S Hopkins III
Aerofax

This book, written by a former USAF RC-135 crew commander, follows the development and service use of this globe-trotting aircraft and its many and varied tasks. Every variant, and sub-variant is charted, the histories of each and every aircraft are to be found within; details of the hundreds of units, past and present, that have flown the Stratotanker are given. This profusely illustrated work will interest those who have flown and serviced them as well as the historian and enthusiast community.

Softback, 280 x 216 mm, 224 pages
210 b/w and 46 colour photos
1 85780 069 9 **£24.95/US $39.95**

**Aerofax**
**YAKOVLEV'S V/STOL FIGHTERS**

John Fricker and Piotr Butowski

Yakovlev's V/STOL Fighters
Yak-36, Yak-38, Yak-41 and Yak-141
The full story of Russia's rivals to the Harrier

The story of Russia's programme to achieve a supersonic VTOL jet fighter can now be revealed, from the earliest Yak-36 'Freehand' experiments through the carrier-operated Yak-38 'Forger' and astonishing Yak-141 'Freehand', on to the agreement between Yakovlev and Lockheed Martin to help produce JAST, the USA's next generation fighter.

Using material never before seen in the West, this book tells the story of a programme that has to an extent, until recently, been shrouded in secrecy.

Softback, 280 x 216 mm, 44 pages
90 b/w photos, diagrams etc
1 85780 041 9 **£7.95/US $12.95**

**Aerofax**
**MiG-21 'FISHBED'**
Most widely used Supersonic Fighter

Yefim Gordon and Bill Gunston

MiG-21 'Fishbed'
The world's most widely used supersonic fighter

Yefim Gordon & Bill Gunston
Aerofax

The ubiquitous MiG-21 is unquestionably one of the greatest fighters of the post-Second World War era. It was Russia's first operational Mach 2-capable interceptor, and a stepping stone for many nations to enter the age of supersonic air combat. Access to the files of the MiG design bureau and other previously inaccessible sources reveal the secrets of the fighter that has flown and fought in more countries than any other supersonic jet.

Softback, 280 x 216 mm, 144 pages
335 b/w and 46 col illusts, plus colour artwork and scale plans.
1 85780 042 7 **£16.95/US $27.95**

**Aerofax**
**MIG-25 'FOXBAT' and MIG-31 'FOXHOUND'**

Yefim Gordon

MiG-25 'Foxbat' MiG-31 'Foxhound'
Russia's defensive front line

Aerofax

This book takes a detailed, informed and dispassionate view of an awesome aeronautical achievement – the titanium and steel MiG-25 – which became the backbone of the USSR defensive structure. Its follow-on was the similar-looking MiG-31 'Foxhound', very much a new aircraft designed to counter US cruise missiles and in production from 1979. Includes a large amount of previously unpublished material plus extensive and lavish illustrations.

Softback, 280 x 216 mm, 96 pages
110 b/w and colour photos plus 91 line and colour airbrush illustrations
1 85780 064 8 **£12.95/US $21.95**

**Aerofax**
**TUPOLEV Tu-95/Tu-142 'BEAR'**

Yefim Gordon and Vladimir Rigmant

Tupolev Tu-95/-142 'Bear'
Russia's Intercontinental-Range Heavy Bomber

Yefim Gordon and Vladimir Rigmant
Aerofax

During the 'Cold War' Tupolev's Tu-95 'Bear' strategic bomber provided an awesome spectacle. It was the mainstay of the USSR's strike force, a reliable and adaptable weapons platform. Additional roles included electronic/photographic reconnaissance and maritime patrol, AEW and command and control.

The author has had unparalleled access to the Tupolev OKB archives, taking the lid off a story previously full of speculation to produce the most comprehensive study to date.

Softback, 280 x 216 mm, 128 pages
236 b/w, 24 col photos, 12 diagrams
1 85780 046 X **£14.95/US $24.95**

# Bibliography

*Air Force Colours Vol 1 ETO and MTO 1942-45:* Dana Bell; Squadron/Signal, USA, 1979.

*Attlebridge Diaries:* John H Woolnough; 8th Air Force News; USA, 1979.

*B-24 Liberator at War:* Roger A Freeman; Ian Allan, UK, 1983.

*B-24 Liberator in Action, Aircraft No.80:* Larry Davis, Squadron/Signal, USA, 1987.

*B-24 Liberator:* Allen G Blue; Ian Allan, UK, 1979.

*B-24 Liberator 1939-45, The:* Martin Bowman; Wensum Books, UK, 1979.

*Bomber Command:* Jeffrey L Ethell; Motorbooks International; USA, 1994.

*Camouflage & Markings - Consolidated B-24 Liberator USAAF ETO & MTO, 1942-45:* Roger A Freeman; Ducimus, UK, 1974.

*Consolidated B-24J Liberator, The - Profile No.19:* Roger A Freeman; Profile Publications, UK, 1965.

*Consolidated B-24 Liberator:* John M & Donna Campbell; Schiffer Military History, USA, 1993

*Eighth Air Force in World War 2:* Kenn C Rust; Historical Aviation Album, USA, 1978.

*Famous Bombers of the Second World War:* William Green; MacDonalds, UK, 1959.

*Fields of Little America:* Martin Bowman; Wensum Books, UK, 1977.

*The Fortunes of War - The 492nd Bomb Group on Daylight Operations:* Allen G Blue; Aero Publishers, USA, 1967.

*History of the 446th Bomb Group, The:* Harold E Jensen; published privately for the 446th Association, USA, 1990.

*Liberator, America's Global Bomber:* Alwyn T Lloyd; Pictorial Histories Publishing, USA, 1993.

*Liberator in Action, Aircraft No.21:* Steve Birdsall; Squadron/Signal, USA, 1975.

*Log of the Liberators:* Steve Birdsall; Doubleday, USA, 1973.

*The Mighty Eighth - A History of the US 8th Army Air Force:* Roger A Freeman; MacDonalds, UK, 1970.

*Mighty Eighth War Diary, The:* Roger A Freeman; Janes, UK, 1981.

*Mighty Eighth War Manual, The:* Roger A Freeman; Janes, UK, 1984.

*Secret Squadrons of the Eighth:* Pat Carty; Ian Allan, UK, 1990.

*Strangers in a Strange Land:* Hans Heiri Stapfer; Squadron/Signal, USA, 1988.

*Strangers in a Strange Land Vol II - Escape to Neutrality:* Hans Heiri Stapfer and Gino Kunzle; Squadron/Signal, USA, 1992.

*US Military Aircraft Designations and Serials 1909 to 1979:* John M Andrade; Midland Counties Publications, UK, reprinted 1997.

*No.458th Bombardment Group, Vols I, II, III and IV:* George A Reynolds; published privately by the author; USA,1996.

*1,000 Day Battle, The:* James Hoseason; Gillingham Publications, UK, 1979.

Above: **The second assembly ship to be used by the 93rd BG was B-24D-165-CO 42-72869, the former *Bear Down*. It carried two wide yellow bands around the nose and rear fuselage.**

Left: **The 44th BG's formation monitor, an early production Republic P-47D Thunderbolt, is seen against a wintry backcloth at Shipdham. Note the serial, positioned on the upper rear fuselage, which although indistinct, is probably '27865', in which case it would have been 42-7865, only the 13th P-47D-1-RE off the production line.**

# Liberator Name Index

It should be remembered that during an aircraft's operational life it could often be subjected to change of tail call-letter, nickname and nose art. Frequently aircraft were transferred to a different squadron within its Group and following major repairs, for instance, an aircraft could be transferred to a different bomb group altogether. Accordingly, this index serves to record the state of aircraft as illustrated on the page(s) concerned and is not a comprehensive listing of all of the B-24s that served within the 2nd Air Division. In similar vein, no attempt has been made to show exact positioning of 'bar' and '+' additions to call-letters and these are presented consistently behind the call-letter, where known. 'The' has been ignored at the beginning of an aircraft's name, and name spellings, punctuation etc are as painted on the aircraft. Only B-24s are indexed.

| Name | Variant | Serial | Letter | Group | Squadron | Page(s) |
|---|---|---|---|---|---|---|
| *Jo-Jo's Special Delivery* | D-1-CO | 41-23683 | | 93rd | | 35 |
| *Johnny Come Lately* | J-140-CO | 42-110154 | 'L+' | 491st | 855th | 72 |
| *Joisey Bounce* | D-25-CO | 41-24226 | 'L–' | 93rd | | 180 |
| *Jug Head* | H-20-DT | 42-51102 | 'P' | 453rd | 732nd | 33 |
| *Katy Bug* | D-1-CO | 41-23745 | 'P' | 93rd | | 91 |
| *Ken-O-Kay* | H-10-FO | 42-52302 | 'C' | 453rd | 732nd | 31 |
| *Kentucky Belle* | J-155-CO | 44-40268 | 'H' | 446th | 706th | 112, 180 |
| *Kill Joy* | H-1-CF | 41-29141 | 'O–' | 446th | | 105 |
| *Laden Maid* | H-15-FO | 42-52560 | | 466th | 786th | 170 |
| *Laden Maid Again* | J | | | 466th | 786th | 148 |
| *Lady Diana II* | J-5-FO | 42-51459 | 'C–' | 392nd | 579th | 70 |
| *Lady Eve* | H-25-FO | 42-95164 | 'P+' | 392nd | 577th | 87 |
| *Lady From Bristol* | H-5-FO | 42-52100 | 'F' | 448th | 714th | 119 |
| *Lady Lightning* | H-15-FO | 42-52597 | | 466th | 784th | 146, 167 |
| *Lady Luck* | H-25-FO | 42-95255 | | 466th | | 150 |
| *Lady Marion* | J-1-FO | 42-50592 | 'N' | 445th | 701st | 42 |
| *Lassie Come Home* | J-155-CO | 44-40283 | | 458th | 753rd | 142, 166 |
| *Last Card Louis* | H-15-FO | 42-52441 | 'I' | 458th | 755th | 136 |
| *Lazy Lou* | H-1-FO | 42-7609 | 'D' | 446th | 706th | 105,109,181 |
| *Lemon Drop* | D-1-CO | 41-23699 | 'P–' | 44th | 68th | 50, 83, 84 |
| *Let'Er Rip* | M-5-FO | 44-50548 | | 466th | 785th | 170 |
| *Liberty Belle* | H-25-DT | 42-51134 | | 466th | 784th | 169 |
| *Liberty Lib* | H-10-CF | 41-29303 | | 458th | 752nd | 165 |
| *Liberty Run* | J-130-CO | 42-110078 | 'P' | 453rd | 735th | 34, 46 |
| *Lil Cookie* | H-1-FO | 42-7552 | 'Z–' | 489th | 845th | 126, 185 |
| *Li'l Gypsy* | H-1-CF | 41-29127 | 'G–' | 392nd | 579th | 64 |
| *Lil' Max* | J-95-CO | 42-100347 | 'M' | 446th | 707th | 107 |
| *Lil Peach* | H-15-CF | 41-29375 | 'A' | 467th | 791st | 154 |
| *Lil Snooks* | H-20-FO | 42-94936 | 'R' | 446th | 707th | 109, 130 |
| *Lillian Ann II* | H-1-FO | 42-7571 | 'D+' | 445th | 700th | 25 |
| *Lily Marlene* | H-25-FO | 42-95260 | 'P' | 44th | 68th | 55 |
| *Linda Mae* | J-5-FO | 42-51075 | 'K' | 448th | | 120 |
| *Little Beaver* | J-150-CO | 44-40194 | 'I+' | 491st | 855th | 73 |
| *Little Gramper* | D-90-CO | 42-40722 | 'B+' | 389th | 566th | 133 |
| | | | | 491st | | 175, 177 |
| *Little Jo* | H-20-CF | 41-28958 | 'P' | 448th | 713th | 119 |
| *Little Joe* | J-145-CO | 44-40084 | 'A–' | 491st | 854th | 88 |
| *Little Lambsy Divey* | J-100-CO | 42-100407 | | 458th | 755th | 139,182,165 |
| *Little Lulu* | H-15-CF | 41-29391 | | 466th | 787th | 169 |
| *Little Rollo* | H-30-FO | 42-95289 | 'N' | 446th | 707th | 6 |
| *Little Sheppard* | H-10-DT | 41-28711 | 'N' | 448th | 712th | 117 |
| *Lonely Heart* | H-25-FO | 42-95224 | | 467th | | 159 |
| *Lonesome Lois* | H-20-FO | 42-95020 | 'X+' | 445th | 701st | 43 |
| *Lonesome Polecat* | H-20-FO | 42-94857 | 'P+' | 489th | 846th | 123 |
| *Lovely Lady's Avenger* | J-145-CO | 44-40093 | | 466th | 786th | 148 |
| *Lover's Lane / Yuvadit* | H-10-CF | 42-64473 | 'R' | 453rd | 735th | 46 |
| *Luck and Stuff* | J-95-CO | 42-100360 | 'B–' | 446th | | 106 |
| *Lucky Gordon* | D-20-CO | 41-24215 | 'Z' | 93rd | | 36 |
| *Lucky Lady Betty II* | H-30-DT | 42-51193 | 'V–' | 389th | 565th | 39 |
| *Lucky Lass* | J-150-CO | 44-40157 | 'L–' | 492nd | 857th | 89 |
| *Lucky 'Leven* | J-20-FO | 44-48820 | | 467th | 791st | 183 |
| *Lucky Tiger* | D-165-CO | 42-72876 | 'R' | 389th | 566th | 38 |
| *Mad Monk* | H-15-CF | 41-29402 | | 458th | 768th | 167 |
| *Mah Aikin Back* | J-150-CO | 44-40226 | 'F–' | 491st | 854th | 88 |
| *Mary Harriet* | J-140-CO | 42-110149 | 'Z' | 453rd | 733rd | 30 |
| *Massillon Tiger* | J-55-CF | 44-10488 | 'B–' | 467th | 789th | 159 |
| *Maulin' Mallard* | J-110-CO | 42-109867 | 'B–' | 93rd | 330th | 129 |
| *Meat Around the Corner* | H-10-DT | 41-28738 | | 458th | 754th | 166 |
| *Merchant of Menace* | J-145-CO | 44-40089 | 'C+' | 491st | 855th | 190 |
| *Merle Lee* | H-1-FO | 42-7584 | | 446th | | 106 |
| *Mighty Mouse* | M-10-FO | 44-50775 | | 446th | 704th | 132 |
| *Minerva* | D-1-CO | 41-23689 | | 44th | 392nd | 82 |
| *Miss America* | J-1-FO | 42-50558 | 'F+' | 389th | 566th | 40 |
| *Miss Fortune* | H-15-FO | 42-52559 | 'R–' | 467th | 790th | 152, 171 |
| *Miss Liberty* | D-165-CO | 42-72871 | 'T+' | 389th | 567th | 37 |
| *Miss Minooky* | H-30-CF | 42-50438 | | 466th | 784th | 147 |
| *Missouri Mauler* | D-20-CF | 42-63980 | 'Q–' | 389th | 567th | 13 |
| *Mistah Chick* | J-75-CO | 42-100146 | 'U' | 389th | 567th | 14, 38 |
| *Mizpah* | J-95-CO | 42-100366 | | 458th | 754th | 137 |
| *Moose* | J-150-CO | 44-40205 | 'G' | 491st | 853rd | 88 |
| *My Buddie* | H-25-FO | 42-95083 | 'A' | 448th | | 121 |
| *My Gal Sal* | J-1-FO | 42-50626 | 'H–' | 44th | 506th | 56 |
| *My Tuffy* | J-75-CO | 42-100167 | 'L+' | 389th | 566th | 16 |
| *Naughty Nan* | H-15-FO | 42-52594 | 'N' | 446th | 705th | 132 |
| *Naughty Nan* | J-55-CO | 42-99949 | 'I' | 93rd | 328th | 98 |
| *Naughty Norma* | J-85-CO | 42-100281 | | 389th | 566th | 38 |
| *Nice N Naughty* | H-1-FO | 42-7476 | 'H' | 44th | 66th | 85 |
| *Nokkish* | H-10-CF | 41-29302 | 'P' | 458th | 752nd | 139, 166 |
| *Nuff Sed* | J-105-CO | 42-109794 | 'S–' | 389th | 565th | 38 |
| *O-Bit-U-Airy-Mary* | J-401-CF | 42-50485 | 'N' | 93rd | 409th | 104 |
| *Ohio Silver* | H-25-FO | 42-95206 | 'J' | 453rd | 732nd | 33, 45 |
| *Ol' Buddy* | H-25-DT | 42-51120 | 'R' | 489th | 844th | 124 |
| *Old Blister Butt* | D-95-CO | 42-40776 | 'H' | 389th | 564th | 12, 37 |
| *Old-Faithful* | H-1-FO | 42-7505 | 'H' | 446th | | 108, 130 |
| *Old Glory* | D-15-CF | 42-63956 | 'X' | 389th | 565th | 39 |
| *Ole Baldy* | H-20-FO | 42-94863 | | 445th | 701st | 42 |
| *Ole Buckshot* | J-1-FO | 42-50739 | 'Z–' | 389th | 567th | 20, 40 |
| *Ole Irish* | D-95-CO | 42-40746 | 'B' | 389th | 564th | 38 |
| *Ole King Cole* | J-1-FO | 42-50565 | 'Q+' | 445th | 700th | 26, 43 |
| *On the Ball* | D-120-CO | 42-40990 | 'L' | 93rd | | 97 |
| *Our Baby* | J-150-CO | 44-40173 | 'K–' | 453rd | 735th | 45 |
| *Our Gal* | J-90-CO | 42-100308 | 'M' | 392nd | 578th | 61, 87 |
| *Paddlefoot* | H-10-DT | 41-28719 | | 458th | 755th | 166 |
| *Paddy's Wagon* | J-145-CO | 44-40114 | 'F+' | 491st | 855th | 78 |
| *Pallas Athene / GI Jane* | J-80-CO | 42-100187 | | 392nd | 578th | 87 |
| *Paper Doll* | H-20-FO | 42-94932 | 'C+' | 489th | 846th | 6 |
| *Parson's Chariot* | J-140-CO | 42-110162 | | 466th | | 148 |
| *Parson's Chariot* | M-10-FO | 44-50699 | | 466th | 784th | 150 |
| *Patches* | H-20-FO | 42-95015 | 'P' | 445th | 700th | 42 |
| *Patches* | J-90-CO | 42-100334 | | 93rd | 409th | 128 |
| *Patriotic Patty* | J-1-FO | 42-50734 | 'B' | 446th | 707th | 113 |
| *Pay Day* | H-15-DT | 41-28938 | | 453rd | 732nd | 46 |
| *Peep Sight* | H-1-FO | 42-7535 | 'U–' | 44th | 506th | 85 |
| *Pegasus* | H-25-DT | 42-51141 | | 466th | | 148 |
| *Perils of Pauline* | H-25-FO | 42-95162 | 'U–' | 467th | 790th | 155, 172 |
| *Pete the POM Inspector* | D-53-CO | 42-40370 | | 467th | | 164 |
| *Pete the POM Inspector 2nd* | H-15-CF | 41-29393 | | 467th | | 164 |
| *Piccadilly Commando* | H-1-CF | 41-29155 | | 446th | 707th | 130 |
| *Piccadilly Lilly* | H-20-CF | 42-50341 | | 448th | 715th | 173 |
| *Piccadilly Pete* | H-10-FO | 42-52118 | 'K' | 448th | 712nd | 180 |
| *Pin Up Girl* | H-20-FO | 42-94941 | 'J+' | 489th | | 174 |
| *Pistol Packin Mama* | D-160-CO | 42-72858 | 'U' | 44th | 68th | 84 |
| *Plate's Date* | H-20-FO | 42-94830 | | 489th | | 175 |
| *Playboy* | H-15-CF | 41-29439 | | 466th | 784th | 168 |
| *Polaris, The Heavenly Body* | H-15-CF | 41-29384 | | 466th | 787th | 168 |
| *Plucky Lucky* | H-20-FO | 42-94820 | 'L–' | 453rd | 735th | 44 |
| *Poop Deck Pappy* | H-1-FO | 42-7521 | 'X' | 392nd | 577th | 62 |
| *Poop Deck Pappy* | H-1-FO | 42-7521 | 'T' | 448th | 714th | 117 |
| *Pregnant Peg* | H-1-FO | 42-7491 | 'R' | 392nd | 577th | 62 |
| *Prince / Princ-ass / Princess* | D-15-CF | 42-63962 | 'W' | 44th | 67th | 49 |
| *Princess Charlotte* | D-5-CO | 41-23769 | 'B' | 44th | 68th | 50 |
| *Princess Konocti* | J-80-CO | 42-100190 | 'J+' | 389th | 566th | 14, 37, 178 |
| *Prowler* | J-75-CO | 42-100171 | | 467th | 790th | 172 |
| *Pugnacious Princess Pat* | J-65-CF | 44-10579 | 'D+' | 389th | 566th | 40 |
| *Puritanical Bitch* | H-30-CF | 42-50427 | 'V' | 44th | 68th | 59 |
| *Queen Marlene* | D-155-CO | 42-72813 | 'L–' | 44th | 66th | 85 |
| *Queen of Hearts* | H-15-FO | 42-52511 | 'E' | 466th | 785th | 168, 182 |
| *Queenie* | J-5-FO | 42-50773 | 'Q' | 446th | 707th | 114 |
| *Rage in Heaven* | J-150-CO | 44-40165 | 'G' | 392nd | 852nd | 73 |
| *Rebel Gal* | H-20-FO | 42-94838 | | 489th | 845th | 124 |
| *Red Ass* | H-25-FO | 42-95203 | 'D' | 446th | 704th | 112, 132 |
| *Reliable Babe* | H-15-FO | 42-52527 | | 466th | 786th | 168 |
| *Rhapsody in Junk* | H-10-DT | 41-28733 | | 458TH | 753rd | 165 |
| *Ronnie* | H-1-CF | 41-29144 | 'P' | 446th | 704th | 109 |
| *Rosalyn* | J-65-CF | 44-10601 | 'A' | 467th | 788th | 160, 172 |
| *Rose of Juarez* | H-1-FO | 42-7469 | 'E–' | 392nd | 579th | 63, 64 |
| *Rough Riders* | H-15-CF | 41-29342 | | | 755th | Front cover |
| *Rugged Buggy* | D-5-CO | 41-23819 | 'A–' | 44th | 68th | 49 |
| *Rugged But Right* | H-20-FO | 42-94953 | 'C' | 448th | 715th | 118, 176 |
| *Rum Dum* | H-20-CF | 42-50280 | 'D–' | 489th | 845th | 124 |
| *Rum Runner* | H-1-DT | 41-28583 | 'F' | 448th | 713th | 118 |
| *Ruptured Duck* | H-15-FO | 42-52770 | 'V' | 392nd | 576th | 68, 87 |
| *Ruth Marie* | J-5-DT | 42-51301 | 'T+' | 453rd | 733rd | 32 |
| *Ruthless Ruthie* | J-155-CO | 44-40317 | 'I–' | 491st | 854th | 81 |
| *Sack* | H-20-FO | 42-94831 | 'D' | 489th | 844th | 124 |
| *Sack Warmer* | H-15-DT | 41-28824 | | 389th | 566th | 39 |
| *Sally* | H-25-FO | 42-95037 | 'M–' | 392nd | 579th | 86, 190 |
| *Satan's Little Sister* | H-25-FO | 42-95180 | | 446th | 706th | 132 |
| *Satan's Mate* | J-95-CO | 42-100341 | 'A' | 458th | 753rd | 135, 165 |
| *Satan's Sister* | H-30-CF | 42-50451 | 'N' | 489th | 844th | 124 |
| *Say When* | J-145-CO | 44-40103 | | 492nd | 858th | 89 |
| *Scrapper* | H-15-FO | 42-52394 | 'F–' | 467th | 790th | 182 |
| *Screamin' Mimi* | D-120-CO | 42-40997 | 'S' | 389th | 564th | 15, 178 |
| *Shack* | J-160-CO | 44-40298 | 'E' | 458th | 754th | 141 |
| *Shack Time* | J-155-CO | 44-40275 | 'L' | 458th | 753rd | 140, 166 |
| *Shadie Sadie* | H-25-FO | 42-95059 | 'O' | 446th | 705th | 115 |
| *Shady Lady* | J-1-FO | 42-50759 | | 448th | | 120 |
| *Sharon D* | H-15-FO | 42-94759 | 'N' | 489th | 845th | 122, 175 |
| *She Devil* | J-145-CO | 44-40123 | 'A' | 491st | 852nd | 76, 88 |
| *Shoot Luke* | D-1-CO | 41-23729 | | 93rd | 328th | 93 |
| *Short Snorter* | J-60-CO | 44-99990 | 'H–' | 392nd | 579th | 63, 179 |
| *Sibonnette* | H-25-FO | 42-95227 | | 389th | 564th | 21, 41 |
| *Silent Yokum* | J-5-FO | 42-50898 | 'V–' | 453rd | 735th | 44 |
| *Silver Chief* | J-150-CO | 44-40201 | 'N' | 492nd | 857th | 143, 175 |
| *Skipper's Clipper* | H-20-FO | 42-95000 | 'Y+' | 445th | 701st | 9 |
| *Slick Chick* | H-25-CF | 42-50388 | 'Z+' | 489th | 846th | 175 |
| *Snafu Snark* | H-15-CF | 41-29387 | | 466th | 785th | 146 |
| *Snooper* | H-15-FO | 42-52571 | | 467th | 790th | 161, 171 |
| *Southern Clipper* | H-15-FO | 42-52546 | | 467th | 790th | 158 |
| *S'O'L* | H | | 'V' | 458th | 753rd | 189 |
| *Southern Comfort* | H-1-FO | 42-7522 | 'S–' | 44th | 506th | 55 |
| *Southern Comfort III* | J-5-FO | 42-50896 | 'R–' | 44th | 506th | 57 |
| *Southern Queen* | D-15-CF | 42-63959 | 'L+' | 389th | 566th | 39 |
| *Spare Parts* | H-5-DT | 41-28654 | | 453rd | 732nd | 31 |
| *Special Delivery* | H-20-FO | 42-94896 | 'C–' | 489th | 845th | 123 |
| *Spirit of Notre Dam* | H-25-FO | 42-95102 | 'H–' | 453rd | 734th | 46 |
| *Spirit of 77* | H-1-FO | 42-7607 | 'O–' | 446th | 705th | 108, 110 |
| *Spotted Ape* | H-20-DT | 41-28967 | | 458th | | 162,163,189 |
| *Squat 'N Droppit* | H-10-DT | 41-28710 | 'M' | 448th | | 173 |
| *Star Dust* | H-1-FO | 42-7576 | 'A–' | 446th | 705th | 105,110,130 |
| *Stormy* | J-1-FO | 42-50574 | 'V' | 445th | 702nd | 26 |
| *Stubby Gal* | H-20-FO | 42-94836 | 'R–' | 489th | 847th | 6 |
| *Sturgeon* | J-130-CO | 42-110066 | | 448th | 715th | 174 |
| *Super Wolf* | H-25-FO | 42-95080 | | 467th | 791st | 172 |
| *Suzy Q* | D-5-CO | 41-23817 | 'L' | 44th | 67th | 48 |
| *Sweat Box* | J-145-CO | 44-40071 | 'D+' | 44th | 66th | 57 |
| *Sweatin it Out* | H-1-FO | 42-7541 | 'A' | 445th | 700th | 41 |
| *Sweetest Rose of Texas* | H-25-DT | 42-51105 | 'O+' | 445th | 701st | 26 |
| *Table Stuff* | J-155-CO | 44-40285 | | 458th | 753rd | 138 |
| *Tahelenback* | H-20-FO | 42-94921 | 'B+' | 445th | 701st | 24, 42 |
| *Tailwind* | H-15-CF | 41-29368 | 'J–' | 467th | 789th | 151 |
| *Tangerine* | H-15-CF | 41-29446 | | 467th | 790th | 152, 171 |

The 458th BG's second assembly ship ***Spotted Ape***, **B-24H-20-DT 41-28967, leads *S'O'L*, from the 753rd BS, together with a 754th BS aircraft, in flight over the Norfolk coast. Note the AZON aerials under the rear fuselage of *S'O'L*.**

**B-24J-95-CO 42-100365 of the 458th BG taken from the waist window of *First Sergeant*, the Group's first assembly ship. The aircraft are overflying the Norfolk coast, with Overstrand visible below the belly of '365. Trimingham railway station is at the bottom of the picture.**

Above: **A famous logo, *Thunderbird* on B-24J-150-CO 44-40238 from the 491st BG's 852nd BS.**

Left: **Coming in to land with the right outboard prop feathered is *Merchant of Menace*, B-24J-145-CO 44-40089 from the 491st BW's 855th BS. She went missing on 13th September 1944.**

Below: **B-24H-25-FO 42-95037 *Sally* of the 392nd BW's 579th BS. *Sally* was salvaged, battle-damaged after a crash landing at Frettenham after the mission to Magdeburg on 29th June 1944.**

# Liberator Serial Index

In this index, aircraft with names are given in place of the call-letter and readers should then refer to the 'By Name' index. Introductory notes as given in the 'By Name' index apply here.

| Serial | Variant | Name or Letter | Group | Sqdn | Page |
|---|---|---|---|---|---|
| 42-7584 | H-1-FO | *Merle Lee* | | | |
| 42-7586 | H-1-FO | 'Q+' | 445th | | 22 |
| 42-7591 | H-1-FO | *Fatstuff II* | | | |
| 42-7607 | H-1-FO | *Spirit of 77* | | | |
| 42-7609 | H-1-FO | *Lazy Lou* | | | |
| 42-7618 | H-1-FO | 'C' | 44th | 66th | 53 |
| 42-7619 | H-1-FO | *Bunnie* | | | |
| 42-7622 | H-1-FO | *Ann* | | | |
| 42-7625 | H-1-FO | 'B–' | 446th | | 106 |
| 42-7655 | H-1-FO | 'P' | 93rd | | 105 |
| 42-7764 | H-5-FO | *Bag of Bolts* | | | |
| 42-72813 | D-155-CO | *Queen Marlene* | | | |
| 42-72857 | D-160-CO | 'X–' | 44th | 506th | 54 |
| 42-72858 | D-160-CO | *Pistol Packin Mama* | | | |
| 42-72866 | D-165-CO | *Jackass Male* | | | |
| 42-72871 | D-165-CO | *Miss Liberty* | | | |
| 42-72876 | D-165-CO | *Lucky Tiger* | | | |
| 42-73477 | J-50-CO | *Feather Merchant* | | | |
| 42-73512 | J-50-CO | 'J' | 448th | | 120 |
| 42-78482 | J-1-NT | 'M+' | 491st | 855th | 74 |
| 42-94783 | H-20-FO | *Jo* | | | |
| 42-94805 | H-20-FO | *Foil Proof* | | | |
| 42-94816 | H-20-FO | *Tiger's Revenge* | | | |
| 42-94820 | H-20-FO | *Plucky Lucky* | | | |
| 42-94828 | H-20-FO | *You're Safe at Home* | | | |
| 42-94829 | H-20-FO | *Bomb Babe* | | | |
| 42-94831 | H-20-FO | *Sack* | | | |
| 42-94836 | H-20-FO | *Stubby Gal* | | | |
| 42-94838 | H-20-FO | *Rebel Gal* | | | |
| 42-94842 | H-20-FO | *Ford's Folly* | | | |
| 42-94857 | H-20-FO | *Lonesome Polecat* | | | |
| 42-94863 | H-20-FO | *Ole Baldy* | | | |
| 42-94896 | H-20-FO | *Special Delivery* | | | |
| 42-94903 | H-20-FO | *Bomber's Moon* | | | |
| 42-94906 | H-20-FO | *Dragon Lady* | | | |
| 42-94921 | H-20-FO | *Tahelenback* | | | |
| 42-94932 | H-20-FO | *Paper Doll* | | | |
| 42-94936 | H-20-FO | *Lil Snooks* | | | |
| 42-94941 | H-20-FO | *Pin Up Girl* | | | |
| 42-94945 | H-20-FO | *Cover Girl* | | | |
| 42-94946 | H-20-FO | *Cats* | | | |
| 42-94953 | H-20-FO | *Rugged But Right* | | | |
| 42-94986 | H-20-FO | *Three Star Special* | | | |
| 42-94992 | H-20-FO | *Dead End Kids* | | | |
| 42-95000 | H-20-FO | *Skipper's Clipper* | | | |
| 42-95010 | H-20-FO | *Crow's Nest* | | | |
| 42-95015 | H-20-FO | *Patches* | | | |
| 42-95016 | H-20-FO | *Down De Hatch* | | | |
| 42-95020 | H-20-FO | *Lonesome Lois* | | | |
| 42-95026 | H-25-FO | *Yankee Rebel* | | | |
| 42-95033 | H-25-FO | 'X–' | 392nd | 578th | 69 |
| 42-95037 | H-25-FO | *Sally* | | | |
| 42-95046 | H-25-FO | 'D' | 93rd | 330th | 103 |
| 42-95050 | H-25-FO | *Gas House Mouse* | | | |
| 42-95057 | H-25-FO | *Angel* | | | |
| 42-95059 | H-25-FO | *Shady Sadie* | | | |
| 42-95063 | H-25-FO | 'B+' | 389th | 566th | 10 |
| 42-95077 | H-25-FO | *Ginny Gal* | | | |
| 42-95080 | H-25-FO | *Super Wolf* | | | |
| 42-95084 | H-25-FO | *Bird Dog* | | | |
| 42-95102 | H-25-FO | *Spirit of Notre Dam* | | | |
| 42-95162 | H-25-FO | *Perils of Pauline* | | | |
| 42-95164 | H-25-FO | *Lady Eve* | | | |
| 42-95180 | H-25-FO | *Satan's Little Sister* | | | |
| 42-95183 | H-25-FO | *Briney Marlin* | | | |
| 42-95184 | H-25-FO | 'P–' | 389th | 567th | 18 |
| 42-95196 | H-25-FO | 'L' | 492nd | 856th | 82 |
| 42-95198 | H-25-FO | *Classy Chassy* | | | |
| 42-95203 | H-25-FO | *Red Ass* | | | |
| 42-95206 | H-25-FO | *Ohio Silver* | | | |
| 42-95218 | H-25-FO | 'T' | 491st | 854th | 74 |
| 42-95224 | H-25-FO | *Lonely Heart* | | | |
| 42-95227 | H-25-FO | *Sibonnette* | | | |
| 42-95248 | H-25-FO | *Falcon* | | | |
| 42-95255 | H-25-FO | *Lady Luck* | | | |
| 42-95260 | H-25-FO | *Lily Marlene* | | | |
| 42-95273 | H-25-FO | | 467th | 790th | 161 |
| 42-95283 | H-25-FO | *Biff Bam* | | | |
| 42-95289 | H-30-FO | *Little Roll* | | | |
| 42-95303 | H-30-FO | *Crows Nest* | | | |
| 42-95308 | H-30-FO | 'C–' | 445th | 702nd | 27 |
| 42-95527 | J-1-FO | *4-F* | | | |
| 42-95592 | J-1-FO | *Black Cat* | | | |
| 42-95610 | J-1-FO | | 458th | 752nd | 143 |
| 42-95619 | J-1-FO | *Bi-U Baby* | | | |
| 42-99949 | J-55-CO | *Naughty Nan* | | | |
| 42-99982 | J-55-CO | | 389th | 566th | 17 |
| 42-100100 | J-70-CO | *Double Trouble* | | | |
| 42-100112 | J-70-CO | 'Q' | 44th | 68th | 53 |
| 42-100146 | J-75-CO | 'E' also *Mistah Chick* | 389th | 564th | 14 |
| 42-100167 | J-75-CO | *My Tuffy* | | | |
| 42-100171 | J-75-CO | *Prowler* | | | |
| 42-100187 | J-80-CO | *GI Jane* also *Pallas Athene* | | | |
| 42-100190 | J-80-CO | *Princess Konocti* | | | |
| 42-100281 | J-85-CO | *Naughty Norma* | | | |
| 42-100284 | J-85-CO | 'L' | 448th | 714th | 116 |
| 42-100294 | J-90-CO | *Victory Belle* | | | |
| 42-100308 | J-90-CO | *Our Gal* | | | |
| 42-100330 | J-90-CO | 'L–' | 44th | 67th | 54 |
| 42-100332 | J-90-CO | *Galloping Katie* | | | |
| 42-100334 | J-90-CO | *Patches* | | | |
| 42-100341 | J-95-CO | *Satan's Mate* | | | |
| 42-100343 | J-95-CO | 'W' | 445th | 703rd | 25 |
| 42-100347 | J-95-CO | *Lil' Max* | | | |
| 42-100353 | J-95-CO | 'L' | 445th | | 25 |
| 42-100357 | J-95-CO | 'O' | 458th | 754th | 137 |
| 42-100360 | J-95-CO | *Luck and Stuff* | | | |
| 42-100365 | J-95-CO | | *458th* | | |
| 42-100366 | J-95-CO | *Mizpah* | | | |
| 42-100404 | J-100-CO | *Grim Reaper* | | | |
| 42-100407 | J-100-CO | *Little Lambsy Divey* | | | |
| 42-100408 | J-100-CO | | 458th | 753rd | 138,176 |
| 42-109792 | J-105-CO | *Wicked Widget III* | | | |
| 42-109794 | J-105-CO | *Nuff Sed* | | | |
| 42-109800 | J-105-CO | 'T' | 44th | 68th | 53 |
| 42-109812 | J-105-CO | 'V' | 458th | 752nd | 139 |
| 42-110072 | J-130-CO | 'L' | 93rd | 330th | 99 |
| 42-110078 | J-130-CO | *Liberty Run* | | | |
| 42-110081 | J-130-CO | *Able Mabel* | | | |
| 42-110084 | J-130-CO | *Don't Cry Baby* | | | |
| 42-110098 | J-135-CO | *Flying Sac* | | | |
| 42-110107 | J-135-CO | *Wham! Bam! Thank You Ma'm* | | | |
| 42-110141 | J-140-CO | *Breezy Lady* | | | |
| 42-110149 | 'J-140-CO | *Mary Harriet* | | | |
| 42-110154 | J-140-CO | *Johnny Come Lately* | | | |
| 42-110162 | J-140-CO | *Parson's Chariot* | | | |
| 42-110163 | J-140-CO | *Time's a' Wastin'* | | | |
| 42-110400 | J-100-CO | 'Y–' | 44th | 506th | 53 |
| 44-10488 | J-55-CF | *Massillon Tiger* | | | |
| 44-10496 | J-55-CF | 'Q+' | 492nd | 859th | |
| 44-10499 | J-55-CO | *Dixie* | | | |
| 44-10510 | J-60-CF | *You Cawn't Miss It* | | | |
| 44-10528 | J-60-CF | *Going My Way* | | | |
| 44-10548 | J-60-CF | 'O+' | 44th | 66th | 57 |
| 44-10552 | J-60-CF | | 467th | 790th | 170 |
| 44-10553 | J-65-CF | 'C' | 44th | 68th | 60 |
| 44-10575 | J-65-CF | *Becoming Back* | | | |
| 44-10579 | J-65-CF | *Pugnacious Princess Pat* | | | |
| 44-10601 | J-65-CF | *Rosalyn* | | | |
| 44-40052 | J-145-CO | 'D–' | 389th | 565th | 18 |
| 44-40068 | J-145-CO | *Umbriago* | | | |
| 44-40071 | J-145-CO | *Sweat Box* | | | |
| 44-40084 | J-145-CO | *Little Joe* | | | |
| 44-40093 | J-145-CO | *Lovely Lady's Avenger* | | | |
| 44-40101 | J-145-CO | *Tubarao* | | | |
| 44-40103 | J-145-CO | *Say When* | | | |
| 44-40113 | J-145-CO | *Gambling Lady* | | | |
| 44-40114 | J-145-CO | *Paddy's Wagon* | | | |
| 44-40117 | J-145-CO | *Hare Power* | | | |
| 44-40120 | J-145-CO | *That's All Brother* | | | |
| 44-40123 | J-145-CO | *She Devil* | | | |
| 44-40124 | J-145-CO | *Uninvited* | | | |
| 44-40125 | J-145-CO | *Herk's Jerks* | | | |
| 44-40137 | J-145-CO | *What's Next Doc?* | | | |
| 44-40157 | J-150-CO | *Lucky Lass* | | | |
| 44-40165 | J-150-CO | *Rage in Heaven* | | | |
| 44-40168 | J-150-CO | *Tequila Daisy* | | | |
| 44-40169 | J-150-CO | *Bottle Baby* | | | |
| 44-40172 | J-150-CO | *Grease Ball* | | | |
| 44-40173 | J-150-CO | *Our Baby* | | | |
| 44-40194 | J-150-CO | *Little Beaver* | | | |
| 44-40238 | J-150-CO | *Thunderbird* | | | |
| 44-40195 | J-150-CO | *Boulder Bluff* | | | |
| 44-40201 | J-150-CO | *Silver Chief* | | | |
| 44-40205 | J-150-CO | *Moose* | | | |
| 44-40213 | J-150-CO | *Jezabelle* | | | |
| 44-40226 | J-150-CO | *Mah Aikin Back* | | | |
| 44-40230 | J-150-CO | *Tung Hoi* | | | |
| 44-40239 | J-150-CO | *Flying Jackass* | | | |
| 44-40241 | J-150-CO | *Hard Way* | | | |
| 44-40249 | J-155-CO | *Back to the Sack* | | | |
| 44-40268 | J-155-CO | *Kentucky Belle* | | | |
| 44-40271 | J-155-CO | *House of Rumour* | | | |
| 44-40273 | J-155-CO | *Howling Banshee* | | | |
| 44-40275 | J-155-CO | *Shack Time* | | | |
| 44-40279 | J-155-CO | *Henry* | | | |
| 44-49279 | L-5-FO | 'F' | 389th | 564th | 19 |
| 44-40283 | J-155-CO | *Lassie Come Home* | | | |
| 44-40285 | J-155-CO | *Table Stuff* | | | |
| 44-40287 | J-155-CO | *Bachelor's Bedlam* | | | |
| 44-40298 | J-160-CO | *Shack* | | | |
| 44-40317 | J-155-CO | *Ruthless Ruthie* | | | |
| 44-40454 | J-165-CO | *Betta Duck* | | | |
| 44-48820 | J-20-FO | *Lucky 'Leven* | | | |
| 44-49355 | L-5-FO | 'L' | 446th | 707th | 6 |
| 44-49582 | L-10-FO | *Fran* | | | |
| 44-49591 | L-10-FO | | 467th | 791st | 157 |
| 44-49610 | L-10-FO | | 467th | 791st | 159 |
| 44-49880 | L-15-FO | 'J' | 93rd | 329th | 180 |
| 44-50490 | M-5-FO | 'A–' | 466th | 787th | 150 |
| 44-50517 | M-5-FO | 'K' | 446th | 707th | 114 |
| 44-50525 | M-5-FO | *Asbestos Alice* | | | |
| 44-50537 | M-5-FO | 'F' | 93rd | 328th | 103 |
| 44-50548 | M-5-FO | *Let 'Er Rip* | | | |
| 44-50573 | M-5-FO | 'L–' | 467th | 789th | 182 |
| 44-50578 | M-5-FO | 'Q–' | 44th | | 58 |
| 44-50579 | M-5-FO | 'C' | 93rd | 328th | 102 |
| 44-50699 | M-10-FO | *Parson's Chariot* | | | |
| 44-50748 | M-10-FO | *Big Headed Kid* | | | |
| 44-50775 | M-10-FO | *Mighty Mouse* | | | |
| 44-50867 | M-15-FO | 'H+' | 389th | 566th | 20 |

**A group of British civilians waves farewell to the crew of a 458th BG-24L as it starts its journey home after VE-Day.**